COURAGE *to* CONQUER

DAVID JEREMIAH

ABOUT
DR. DAVID JEREMIAH
AND TURNING POINT

D r. David Jeremiah is the founder of Turning Point, a ministry committed to providing Christians with sound Bible teaching relevant to today's changing times through radio and television broadcasts, audio series, books, and live events. Dr. Jeremiah's common-sense teaching on topics such as family, prayer, worship, angels, and biblical prophecy forms the foundation of Turning Point.

David and his wife, Donna, reside in El Cajon, California, where he serves as the senior pastor of Shadow Mountain Community Church. David and Donna have four children and twelve grandchildren.

In 1982, Dr. Jeremiah brought the same solid teaching to San Diego television that he shares weekly with his congregation. Shortly thereafter, Turning Point expanded its ministry to radio. Dr. Jeremiah's inspiring messages can now be heard worldwide on radio, television, and the Internet.

Because Dr. Jeremiah desires to know his listening audience, he travels nationwide holding ministry events that touch the hearts and lives of many people. According to Dr. Jeremiah, "At some point in time, everyone reaches a turning point; and for every person, that moment is unique, an experience to hold onto forever. There's so much changing in today's world that sometimes it's difficult to choose the right path. Turning Point offers people an understanding of God's Word as well as the opportunity to make a difference in their lives."

Dr. Jeremiah has authored numerous books, including *Escape the Coming Night* (Revelation), *The Handwriting on the Wall* (Daniel), *Overcoming Loneliness, God in You* (Holy Spirit), *31 Days to Happiness — Searching for Heaven on Earth, Captured by Grace, Agents of the Apocalypse, RESET—Ten Steps to Spiritual Renewal, Ten Questions Christians Are Asking, A Life Beyond Amazing, Perhaps Today, Overcomer, The Book of Signs, Shelter in God,* and *Forward.*

How to Use This Study Guide

The purpose of this Turning Point study guide is to reinforce Dr. David Jeremiah's dynamic, in-depth teaching and to aid the reader in applying biblical truth to his or her daily life. This study guide is designed to be used in conjunction with Dr. Jeremiah's *Courage to Conquer* audio series, but it may also be used by itself for personal or group study.

Structure of the Lessons

Each lesson is based on one of the messages in the *Courage to Conquer* compact disc series and focuses on specific passages in the Bible. Each lesson is composed of the following elements:

- *Outline*

The outline at the beginning of the lesson gives a clear, concise picture of the topic being studied and provides a helpful framework for readers as they listen to Dr. Jeremiah's teaching.

- *Overview*

The overview summarizes Dr. Jeremiah's teaching on the passage being studied in the lesson. Readers should refer to the Scripture passages in their own Bibles as they study the overview. Unless otherwise indicated, Scripture verses quoted are taken from the New King James Version.

- *Personal and Group Application Questions*

This section contains a variety of questions designed to help readers dig deeper into the lesson and the Scriptures, and to apply the lesson to their daily lives. For Bible study groups or Sunday school classes, these questions will provide a springboard for group discussion and interaction.

- *Did You Know?*

This section presents a fascinating fact, historical note, or insight that adds a point of interest to the preceding lesson.

Personal Study

Thank you for selecting *Courage to Conquer* for your current study. The lessons in this study guide were created to help you gain fresh insights into God's Word and develop new perspectives on topics you may have previously studied. Each lesson is designed to challenge your thinking and help you grow in your knowledge of Christ. During your study, it is our prayer that you will discover how biblical truth affects every aspect of your life and your relationship with Christ will be strengthened.

When you commit to completing this study guide, try to set apart a time, daily or weekly, to read through the lessons without distraction. Have your Bible nearby when you read the study guide, so you're ready to look up verses if you need to. If you want to use a notebook to write down your thoughts, be sure to have that handy as well. Take your time to think through and answer the questions. If you plan on reading the study guide with a small group, be sure to read ahead and be prepared to take part in the weekly discussions.

Leader's Guide

Thank you for your commitment to lead a group through *Courage to Conquer*. Being a leader has its own rewards. You may discover that your walk with the Lord deepens through this experience. Throughout the study guide, your group will explore new topics and review study questions that encourage thought-provoking group discussion.

The lessons in this study guide are suitable for Sunday school classes, small-group studies, elective Bible studies, or home Bible study groups. Each lesson is structured to provoke thought and help you grow in your knowledge and understanding of God. There are multiple components in this section that can help you structure your lessons and discussion time, so make sure you read and consider each one.

Before You Begin

Before you begin each meeting, make sure you and your group are well-versed with the content of the chapter. Every person should have his or her own study guide so they can follow along and write in the study guide if need be. When possible, the study guide should be used with the corresponding compact disc series. You may wish to assign the study guide lesson as homework prior to the meeting of the group and then use the meeting time to listen to the CD and discuss the lesson.

To ensure that everyone has a chance to participate in the discussion, the ideal size for a group is around eight to ten people. If there are more than ten people, try to break up the bigger group into smaller subgroups. Make sure the members are committed to participating each week, as this will help create stability and help you better prepare the structure of the meeting.

At the beginning of the study each week, start the session with a question to challenge group members to think about the issues you will be discussing. The members can answer briefly, but the goal is to have an idea in their mind as you go over the lesson. This allows the group members to become engaged and ready to interact with the group.

After reviewing the lesson, try to initiate a free-flowing discussion. Invite group members to bring questions and insights they may have discovered to the next meeting, especially if they were unsure of the meaning of some parts of the lesson. Be prepared to discuss how biblical truth applies to the world we live in today.

Weekly Preparation

As the group leader, here are a few things you can do to prepare for each meeting:

- Choose whether or not you will play the CD message during your small group session.

  If you decide to play the CD message from Dr. Jeremiah as part of the meeting, you will need to adjust the group time accordingly.

- Make sure you are thoroughly familiar with the material in the lesson.

  Make sure you understand the content of the lesson so you know how to structure group time and you are prepared to lead group discussion.

- Decide, ahead of time, which questions you plan to discuss.

  Depending on how much time you have each week, you may not be able to reflect on every question. Select specific questions which you feel will evoke the best discussion.

- Take prayer requests.

  At the end of your discussion, take prayer requests from your group members and pray for each other.

FOR CONTINUING STUDY

For a complete listing of Dr. Jeremiah's materials for personal and group study call 1-800-947-1993, go online to www.DavidJeremiah.org, or write to Turning Point, P.O. Box 3838, San Diego, CA 92163.

Dr. Jeremiah's *Turning Point* program is currently heard or viewed around the world on radio, television, and the Internet in English. *Momento Decisivo*, the Spanish translation of Dr. Jeremiah's messages, can be heard on radio in every Spanish speaking country in the world. The television broadcast is also broadcast by satellite throughout the Middle East with Arabic subtitles.

Contact Turning Point for radio and television program times and stations in your area, or visit our website at www.DavidJeremiah.org/stationlocator.

COURAGE TO CONQUER

H erman Wouk, the acclaimed American Jewish novelist, recounts in *The Will to Live On* a 1955 meeting he had with the first president of the modern state of Israel, David Ben-Gurion. Wouk and his wife visited the former president at his home in Israel's Negev Desert. They were escorted there by soldiers in a jeep with a mounted machine gun—the newly-formed country was under constant attack by *fedayeen*, terrorists from Egypt and Gaza.

After hours of conversation, the Wouks prepared to leave; and Ben-Gurion cut to the chase: "You must return here to live," he said. "This is the only place for Jews like you. Here you will be free."

"Free?" Wouk replied. "Free? With enemy armies ringing you, with their leaders publicly threatening to wipe out 'the Zionist entity,' with your roads impassable after sundown— *free*?"

"I did not say *safe*," the elder statesman retorted. "I said *free*."

Which would you rather be—safe or free? Along the same line, which would you rather be—courageous or never threatened? Courageous or never doubting? Courageous or never challenged? Courageous or never alone? Courageous or never weary? Sometimes in life we wish for the wrong things.

Ben-Gurion had it right: We are not promised a life of complete safety. He had been through too much in birthing a new nation to believe that. And the writers of Scripture had it right as well: God has not promised us a life totally free from threats, discomfort, fear, loneliness, or disappointment. What God has promised is a life filled with courage to face everything that threatens our stability, our freedom, and our joy.

Courage to Conquer is a study guide written to build you up in your spiritual birthright, confidence in God that leads to courage in life. This series of lessons is based on a sure truth: It is not a question of *if* your peace and stability will be challenged in life, but *when*. Therefore, forewarned is forearmed if you will take to heart what the Scriptures teach about how to have courage to conquer whatever life brings your way.

If ever there was a time and place to seek courage from the Lord, it would be now on planet Earth. Wars and rumors of wars . . . threats of biological and other forms of terrorism . . . economic uncertainty . . . geo-political instability.

What do you do when fear raises its ugly head? One section of my Bible that is well-worn is Psalm 34. It is a sanctuary for all who experience the fears that make the rounds in the world we live in. As Christians, we are not immune to fear. It seeks us out and finds us like it does any other person. But, as Christians, we do not have to dwell in fear. We can learn from the author of Psalm 34 how he dealt with fear and kept it from dominating his life.

There are fourteen psalms in the Old Testament that are linked to specific events in David's life, usually found in those psalms' superscriptions (just under the number of the psalm in most English Bibles). Psalm 34's superscription reads, "A psalm of David when he pretended madness before Abimelech, who drove him away, and he departed." Without this note, we would not know the source of David's fear. But with it, we know it refers to events in David's life described in 1 Samuel 21–22.

You probably know the stories associated with David's rise to prominence in Israel. They begin with his defeat of the Philistine giant, Goliath (1 Samuel 17). David went out to meet the giant in battle armed with nothing but his sling and the name of the Lord. When he killed the giant and cut off his head, he became an immediate teenage hero in Israel: "So the women sang as they danced, and said: 'Saul has slain his thousands, and David his ten thousands'" (1 Samuel 18:7). This adoration caused Saul, the king of Israel at the time, to be enraged with jealousy over David's popularity.

For several years David lived his life as a man on the run, always looking over his shoulder to see if Saul was about to kill him. At one point, Saul commissioned thirty thousand soldiers to seek out David and end his life. During this period, David depended on God to protect him from the murderous Saul. He cried out to God for protection and direction and strength. But, as someone once wrote, "Fatigue makes cowards of us all." And fatigue got the best of David at one point.

David and some of his men fled to the Philistine city of Gath to hide from Saul—the home of Goliath whom David had killed! Not a smart thing to do, especially since he showed up carrying the sword of Goliath that he had gotten from a priest in the village of Nob on the way to Gath. To put this in colloquial terms, any time we stop trusting in God—either due to fatigue or fear or carnality —we start doing really dumb things. And that's exactly what David was doing at this point in his life.

Upon arriving in Gath, David was immediately identified. When David realized the people knew who he was, he did a bizarre thing: He feigned madness—started acting like he was insane (1 Samuel 21:11-15). When David was taken to Achish, the king of Gath, drooling and acting insane, Achish threw him out: "Have I need of madmen, that you have brought this fellow to play the madman in my presence? Shall this fellow come into my house?" (verse 15)

David's ploy worked, and he escaped unharmed to the cave of Adullam.

Now—let's refer again to the superscription of Psalm 34: "A Psalm of David when he pretended madness before Abimelech, who drove him away, and he departed." So this psalm provides a look into the heart and soul of a man who was fleeing for his life at a point where his fatigue and fear had caused him to act completely unbecomingly. (Note: The word *Abimelech* in the superscription refers to Achish. *Abimelech* was a titular word, meaning "king" or "ruler," not a name. So Abimelech Achish meant King Achish.)

Instead of remaining dependent on the Lord while being hounded by Saul, David became a freelancer—doing his own thing. Hiding in enemy territory . . . acting like an insane person— this was not behavior consistent with a "man after [God's] own heart" (Acts 13:22). When David stood before Goliath, he was standing in the middle of God's will. When he stood before Achish, he was standing in the middle of his own will. He probably thought he was a dead man when he realized he'd been identified in Gath as the one who killed Goliath. He had sunk to the lowest point in his young life by the time he reached the cave of Adullam. Promised the throne of Israel by God, he was being hunted down like a common criminal by the king he was supposed to replace. He was consumed with frustration and fear—and Psalm 34 is the record of how he got his spiritual act together again.

Psalm 34 is lengthy (22 verses), and we can't cover it all in one lesson of this study guide. So we will focus on the first seven verses where we will discover four principles for dealing with fear, straight from the pen of one who knew what it was like to be afraid.

WE NEED COURAGE TO OFFER UP OUR PRAISE

If you are one who makes notes in your Bible, I encourage you to underline the five phrases in verses 1-3 that David employs when he moves from the pain of his life to the praise of his lips: "I will bless the Lord at all times". . . "His praise shall continually be in my mouth". . . "My soul shall make its boast in the Lord". . . "Oh, magnify the Lord". . ."Let us exalt His name together."

It's easy to sing a song of praise in the day of prosperity, but David is singing a song of praise in the dark night of his soul. He says that God's praise will continually be—note this—not just in his heart but in his mouth. He is praising the Lord out loud to those who are with him in the cave.

The reason this is significant is that David is choosing—choosing!—to praise God even though there is no way he could have emotionally felt like doing so. He demonstrates that there is no time that demands praise more than at the moment we think we are sinking beneath the surface. That's the time to lift up our arms and open our mouths and put the praise of the Lord on our lips.

Some people say they can't praise the Lord because they don't feel like it. But life is not about feeling good, it's about doing good. And the times when we don't feel good are the exact times we should choose, as act of our will, to offer praise to God. The first step to leaving fear behind is to praise the Lord.

When we praise God in the midst of our fears, the cause of our fear does not go away, nor does the fear itself. What happens is that our fear assumes its proper perspective against the backdrop of the majesty and awesomeness of God. Our fears are shown in their true size—small!—compared to the size of our God: huge! Do you recall the first words of the prayer Jesus taught His disciples to pray? "Hallowed be thy name" (Matthew 6:9, KJV). That prayer begins with praise because praise establishes God in His rightful place as bigger than the source of any of our needs or fears.

So David is saying, "Lord, I've messed up and gotten myself in a fix. But I'm now going to turn my eyes back upon You and praise You for who You are."

WE NEED COURAGE TO OWN OUR PROBLEM

After praising and worshiping God to get our fears in perspective, the second thing we need to do (the second thing David did) is to own our fears—that is, admit them before God. David says, "I sought the Lord, and He heard me, and delivered me from all my fears" (verse 4).

I believe that even while David was feigning madness in Gath, he was crying out to the Lord for deliverance: "Have mercy, Lord! Help me, Lord! I know I'm wrong, Lord, but please help me. I don't know what I'm doing, but, Lord, help me. I'm going to die here, Lord, if You don't help me! Lord, I'm telling You, I'm afraid!"

In spite of the fact that David was wrong, God stepped in "and delivered [him] from all [his] fears" (verse 4). God's mercy is like none other's. Had David been crying out to me, I would have said, "David, you got yourself into this mess—you get yourself out of it. You walked away from my counsel. You played the stupid game of embarrassing me. Here you're the king-in-waiting, and you're walking around with saliva dripping off your beard. You came into this situation; you get out of this situation." Unlike I would have been, God was merciful and delivered David from his fears. Aren't you glad that you can call out to God, even when you are failing with fear, and He will hear and deliver you?

And note what David calls himself in verse six: "This poor man." Not "this strong man," but "this poor man." David had no food, no sword, no army, no throne. He was an anointed king, but not an inaugurated king. He had nothing and no one (except a few companions) but God. He was weak, poor, afraid, and guilty of false pretense. David was calling out in the middle of his weakness just as the apostle Paul did in 2 Corinthians 12:10: "For when I am weak, then I am strong." Paul learned that it took weakness on our part to experience God's power in our life. David tried to be strong in Gath and ended up weak. And that's when God intervened and lifted him up once again. David, a poor man, cried out to his rich God, and God heard him. He owned his problems; he admitted his poverty. That put David in the perfect place to get help from God.

When you find yourself overcome with fear—even if it's you that caused the situation you're in—start by praising God for who He is compared to what your problem is. Second, own your problem.

Don't try to pass it off on someone else. Confess where you are, how you got there, and what you need God to do for you. God will do for you what He did for David. He will deliver you from all your fears.

WE NEED COURAGE TO OVERCOME THROUGH PRAYER

After praise and confession (ownership) of his situation, David turned to serious prayer: "This poor man cried out, and the Lord heard him, and saved him out of all his troubles" (verse 6).

Throughout this psalm, we find words related to David's intense style of prayer: "sought" (verse 4), "cried" (verse 6), "seek" (verse 10), and "cry out" (verse 17). David did not come to the Lord with hesitancy. He is a model of what we find in Hebrews 4:16—coming boldly to the throne of grace to "obtain mercy and find grace to help in time of need." Too many Christians have bought into the error that we cannot call out to God when we feel guilty or ashamed of our condition. But that is exactly when we should pray— intensely and boldly!

It doesn't matter who you are—you can find yourself consumed with fear. Even pastors can be fearful. Many pastors' confidence levels fluctuate with the attitude and size of their congregation. To defend themselves against fear, they may begin to compromise their positions or values in order to keep people happy and keep their church growing. But that is the same as the fleshly strategy David employed to protect himself in Gath. And that is not a way to defeat fear.

Here are some wise words about defeating fear from a pastor who wrestled with the challenge:

> In my struggle with the fear of man, I began to see how fear had subverted my confidence in God. He had been dethroned in my life; people had taken His place. I was no longer trusting God; I was fearing church boards and ministry heads instead. Since fear of man cedes power to human beings that rightfully belongs to God, it is actually a form of idolatry. When we are ruled by the fear of man —as I was—those we're afraid of usurp God's sovereign place in our lives.[1]

When we fear someone other than God, that person becomes our god. That person is the last person we think of at night and the first person we think of in the morning. But that's who God is supposed to be in our lives! So fear has caused us to make someone besides God number one in our life. When we find ourselves in that situation, we have to turn back to God and say, "Lord God, please forgive me. I'll be back again, I'm sure, because this thing isn't going to go away today. But I want You to know, I've got it in perspective. I know, because I let fear control me, I've stopped letting You be the Lord of my life."

It is only as we overcome through prayer that fear can be reduced by trust. For those who have lived under the yoke of fear for a long time, learning to trust God can be a struggle. But if you are a Christian, and you believe God can take you to heaven, then you can also believe God can deliver you from fear.

WE NEED COURAGE TO OBTAIN GOD'S PROVISION

We need courage to praise, to own our problem, and to pray. Finally, we need courage to obtain God's provision. And God's provision is two-fold: It involves deliverance and a Deliverer.

God's Provision Involves Deliverance

I love Psalm 34 because it is all about a solution to a problem. David has a problem and he finds a solution: deliverance! I counted at least six times in this psalm where the words "save" or "deliver" occur. That's what the psalm is all about.

- Verse 4: "He heard me, and delivered me from all my fears."
- Verse 6: "The Lord heard him, and saved him out of all his troubles."
- Verses 17-18: "The righteous cry out, and the Lord hears, and delivers them out of all their troubles. The Lord is near to those who have a broken heart, and saves such as have a contrite spirit."
- Verse 19: "Many are the afflictions of the righteous, but the Lord delivers him out of them all."

If we seek Him, He will deliver us (verse 4). If we look, He will shine His light on us (verse 5). If we cry, He will save us (verse 6). If we fear, He will surround us (verse 7). All He asks is that we trust Him (verse 8), fear Him (verse 9), and seek Him (verse 10). He asks us to let Him replace fear in our life so fear is no longer the dominant factor.

God's Provision Involves a Deliverer

Deliverance only happens when there is a Deliverer. So the Deliverer is really more important than the deliverance itself.

We often hear verse 7 in this psalm quoted: "The angel of the Lord encamps all around those who fear Him, and delivers them." There are only three references in the psalms to the "angel of the Lord": once here in Psalm 34 and twice in Psalm 35. The term "angel of the Lord" is what theologians refer to as a Christophany: a preincarnate appearance of the Lord Jesus Christ. That is, an appearance of Christ in the Old Testament prior to His incarnation in human flesh.

Christ was born into this world in Bethlehem as described in Luke 2. But that was not the beginning of Christ. He has been Christ from eternity past and will be Christ into eternity future. The term "the angel of the Lord" is a term that only occurs prior to the coming of Christ since after His incarnation a Christophany would no longer be needed. In the Old Testament the angel of the Lord appeared to meet certain needs (Genesis 22:11, 15) and that is what He did in David's case—He appeared to deliver David from fear: "The angel of the Lord encamps around those who fear him, and delivers them" (Psalm 34:7, NRSV).

In 2 Kings 6 we have a story of what it means to have the forces of heaven encamped all around you to deliver you from fear. The prophet Elisha and his servant had been ministering on behalf of Israel to protect Israel from the armies of Syria. Elisha and his servant were in Dothan when they woke up one morning and found themselves surrounded by the enemy. The servant of Elisha was consumed with fear when he walked out and saw the armies of Syria poised for attack: "Alas, my master! What shall we do?" (verse 15) Here is what Elisha replied: "Do not fear, for those who are with us are more than those who are with them" (verse 16).

Elisha's servant must have thought his master was seeing things —and he was! The heavens were filled with horses and chariots of fire ready to come to Elisha's defense. But his servant couldn't see them. So Elisha prayed that God would open his servant's eyes so he could see the hosts of heaven encamped around them. Not only was Elisha's servant delivered from fear, the Syrian armies were struck with blindness so that their attack failed.

This is what David experienced in the cave of Adullam. His spiritual eyes were opened, and he saw the angel of the Lord camped around him, and he was delivered from his fears and behavior.

And the same thing can happen to you. If you're lying in a hospital bed waiting on the results of a test or surgery, not knowing what the future holds, fear can grip your heart like a vise. But those who fear the Lord more than they fear death or discomfort or any other life-changing event will find the hosts of heaven camped around their bed to deliver them from fear.

When bad news comes and you don't know what to do, call out and ask the Lord to draw near to you. And the angel of the Lord, our Lord Jesus Christ, will encamp around you and give you His peace whatever the situation (Philippians 4:6-7). Begin to offer up praise to the Lord, be willing to own your problem, call out to God in prayer, and then look for God's provision of deliverance through the Deliverer.

Ask God to open your eyes and let you see His presence. When you compare the source of your fear with God . . . well, there is no comparison. All who fear Him will be delivered.

Note

1. Dave Shive, "You've Got to Fear Somebody," *Discipleship Journal*, Issue 130, July/August 2002.

1. Read 1 Samuel 21:1-15.

   a. What weapon did Ahimelech the priest give to David? (verse 9)

   b. Whom was David fleeing from? (verse 10)

   c. Who recognized David, and why was this dangerous for him? (verse 11)

   d. What did David do once he was recognized? (verse 13)

   e. How did Achish the king of Gath respond to David's ploy? (verses 14-15)

   f. Where does David head after the incident in Gath? (See 1 Samuel 22:1.)

2. Read Psalm 34.

   a. At what point in his life did David write this psalm?

   b. How does knowing the context of when this psalm was written help you understand it better?

   c. List the five phrases that David used in verses 1-3 to express his worship to God.

   d. What do these verses teach you about the importance of worshiping God in the midst of difficulties?

   e. According to verse 4, what did David do? And what did God do?

d. How does worshiping God when we are afraid help put our fear into perspective?

e. What words in this psalm demonstrate the intensity of David's prayer? (See verses 4, 6, 10, and 17.)

f. Discuss how David's prayer models the instructions about prayer found in Hebrews 4:16.

g. If comfortable, share with the group a time when you feared a person and allowed them to become more important in your life than God. Share how that impacted your everyday life and how you put God back in His rightful place in your life.

h. In what two ways does God provide for us when we are battling fear?

i. List the phrases where "save" or "deliver" occur in this psalm.

- _____. (verse 4)

- _____. (verse 6)

- _____. (verse 7)

- _____. (verse 17)

- _____. (verse 18)

- _____. (verse 19)

3. Read Philippians 4:6-7 as a group.

   a. What are we to do when we are anxious? (verse 6)

   b. What is the result when we take these actions? (verse 7)

Whether intentionally or not, President Franklin Roosevelt set forth a biblical premise when he said, "The only thing we have to fear is . . . [dramatic pause in his speech] fear itself!" He made the statement in his first inaugural address in 1933. The Great Depression had reached its worst state, and America was fearful that the nation was on the brink of collapse. Roosevelt used his speech as an opportunity to rally the nation, calling fear a "nameless, unreasoning, unjustified terror which paralyzes needed efforts to convert retreat into advance." He employed numerous biblical images in his speech, referring to "plagues of locusts" and "money-changers in the temple," calling on God at the end for His protection and blessing.

COURAGE WHEN FAITH DESERTS YOU

Romans 8:35-39

In this lesson we learn that nothing can separate us from the love of God.

OUTLINE

What kinds of events make you feel as if God's love has been withdrawn? Perhaps the loss of a relationship, the death of a loved one, or a financial reversal is enough to make you feel unloved. The Bible says that there is nothing that can stop the ever-present reality of God's love for you.

I. **Take Courage From the Strength of God's Love**
   A. God's Love Is Stronger Than the Pressures That You Face
   B. God's Love Is Stronger Than Pain
   C. God's Love Is Stronger Than Persecution
   D. God's Love Is Stronger Than Privation
   E. God's Love Is Stronger Than Poverty
   F. God's Love Is Stronger Than Peril
   G. God's Love Is Stronger Than Prison

II. **Take Courage From the Success of God's Love**

III. **Take Courage From the Safety of Christ's Love**
   A. Not the Crisis of Death nor the Calamities of Life
   B. Not the Intervention of Angels nor the Intrusion of Demons
   C. Not the Cares of Today nor the Concerns of Tomorrow
   D. Not the Inflictions From Heaven nor the Advances of Hell
   E. Not Anything Actual or Possible

Perhaps you've had a crisis loom in your life that you couldn't understand—an illness, the loss of a job, or the death of a loved one. It was a complete shock to your spiritual system, not something you were prepared for. At first you prayed, read your Bible, and tried to remain faithful to God. But in time, your faith began to wane. Where was God? Why wasn't He healing you . . . providing a new job . . . comforting you? Soon, maybe your faith began to fail you. And soon, you didn't feel like much of a Christian at all. You felt like a person living life with no faith at all.

What do you do when your faith deserts you? It can happen; we are not perfect. We would not be provided great truths about God in the Scriptures to build up our faith if there was no possibility that our faith would ever fail.

The apostle Paul had obviously given much thought to the subject of God's love and how it never fails us—how we are never separated from His love regardless of how things might appear. In Romans 8:35-39 Paul tells us how to find courage when we feel God has forgotten us, when we feel our faith deserting us and leaving us on our own. He tells us we can take courage from the strength, success, and safety of God's love.

TAKE COURAGE FROM THE STRENGTH OF GOD'S LOVE

I believe what lies behind Paul's words in verses 35-36 is his own experience as an apostle of Christ. All the things he mentions —tribulation, distress, persecution, famine, nakedness, peril, sword—were things he had endured for the sake of Jesus. And through all that, he had never been separated from God's love for him.

God's Love Is Stronger Than the Pressures That You Face

The word "tribulation" is a word that means to be squeezed; to be put under pressure. This word occurs many times in the New Testament in different contexts, but the basic meaning always has to do with pressure. Paul is saying there is no pressure strong enough to push you beyond the reach of God's love.

God's Love Is Stronger Than Pain

When Paul refers to "distress," he uses a word that actually means a very narrow place. Think of being forcibly pushed through a very narrow opening and the pain and discomfort that would bring. There is no distress—no place so narrow—that you will be separated from God's love.

God's Love Is Stronger Than Persecution

To be persecuted in the New Testament means to be pursued; to be chased down and harassed or harmed because of your testimony for Christ. In Matthew 5:10 Jesus said, "Blessed are those who are persecuted for righteousness' sake, for theirs is the kingdom of heaven." The Bible says that if you live in a godly way for the sake of Christ, you will be persecuted (2 Timothy 3:12). But Paul says that no matter how far you are chased for Christ's sake, you will never be beyond the reach of God's love.

God's Love Is Stronger Than Privation

The famine Paul refers to here is usually privation resulting from faithfulness to Christ, not from a natural famine. Even when you are faithful to Christ and are fired from your job because of it and you can't put food on the table, God's love is with you.

God's Love Is Stronger Than Poverty

"Nakedness" is not a reference to nudity, it is a result of being so poverty-stricken that you can't afford to buy decent clothing (1 Corinthians 4:11). Whatever the reason for your situation of poverty, you will be tempted to be embarrassed and wonder why God doesn't deliver you out of your situation. But Paul says that our clothing has nothing to do with the way God loves us. We have His love even if we have little else.

God's Love Is Stronger Than Peril

Paul was an expert on peril. In one verse in 2 Corinthians 11, Paul uses the word "peril" eight times: "In journeys often, in perils of waters, in perils of robbers, in perils of my own countrymen, in perils of the Gentiles, in perils in the city, in perils in the wilderness, in perils in the sea, in perils among false brethren" (verse 26). If you wanted to find Paul, the best place to look was in the local jail because he was always in peril of being jailed for preaching the Gospel. Paul was in jeopardy every hour of his life (1 Corinthians 15:30). Still he was never separated from the love of Christ.

Not the Inflictions From Heaven nor the Advances of Hell

The present and future reflect Paul's statement about the linear continuum of time—the horizontal perspective of protection. "Nor height nor depth" reflects his comfort in God's protection along the vertical line. Nothing from the highest heaven to the depths of the earth can separate us from the love of God.

Not Anything Actual or Possible

Paul concludes his litany of possibilities with one dramatic statement: "nor any other created thing." That covers it all! Since God created everything in the universe, everything is less powerful than God—everything! Every created thing means anything, actual or possible, in the universe. Therefore, there is nothing that can separate us from the love of God in Christ Jesus. Paul makes this final sweeping statement to cover anything and everything that anyone might think was unique to their situation: "But Paul, what about . . . ?" There is nothing in my life or in yours that is not a "created thing." Nothing can separate us from His love.

So, here is the practical application from this passage in Romans 8. The very next time you think God has forgotten you and your faith is deserting you, pull out Paul's list and see if your situation falls under one of Paul's categories. I can already tell you it will. There are no loopholes, no room for anything to slip by God's protection and separate you from His love.

Here is the second application. There *will* be times when you feel this way in the future—I am warning you now. I don't mean to accuse you of being weak in faith. I am simply reminding you that we live in a world that, from a human perspective, is unstable and insecure. Christians are not guaranteed immunity from temptation, problems, and tragedies. You will have times when you wonder where God is . . . why He is not protecting you . . . why your faith doesn't seem adequate to bring God closer to you. So, prepare yourself now for those times. Center your mind on the truth of what Paul has written here: There is nothing that can separate you from the love of God which is in Christ Jesus our Lord.

But here's a subtle distinction to keep in mind. Our confidence is not in our love for God. Our love for God is fickle and faltering. We would not want to depend for our protection upon our own frail faith. Rather, our confidence is in God Himself and His love for us. Because He is the same yesterday, today, and tomorrow

(Hebrews 13:8), we know that His love is the same as well—His love being an attribute that does not change.

George Matheson was born in Glasgow, Scotland, in 1842. As a child, he had only partial vision; and his sight became progressively worse until it resulted in blindness by the time he was eighteen. But despite his handicap, he was a brilliant student. He studied at the University of Glasgow and later graduated from seminary. He pastored several churches in Scotland including a large church in Edinburgh where he was greatly respected and loved.

He had been engaged to marry a young woman; but she suddenly broke off the engagement, saying she could never be happy married to a blind man. Matheson was crushed. I can imagine this was a time when he wondered why God had allowed him to be so hurt. But he did not wonder long. He soon penned the beautiful hymn, "O Love That Wilt Not Let Me Go:"

> O love that wilt not let me go,
> I rest my weary soul in thee;
> I give thee back the life I owe
> That in thine ocean depths its flow
> May richer, fuller be.[3]

The fickle love of a fiancée let George Matheson go, but the love of God would not let him go. Perhaps more people are hurt by relationships than any other cause. People will fail us, and we ourselves might be the cause of a painful relationship. But there is one relationship that will never hurt us, one that will never let us go: our relationship with God. Even if we are not able to hold on to God, God will hold on to us (2 Timothy 2:13). When you face difficulties, don't say, "I've got to love God more." Instead, get in the Word of God and discover again how much God loves you!

The most important part of realizing and walking in the love of God in Christ is to be *in Christ*. It is only those who have placed their faith in Him who can enter the secure relationship of love that the Heavenly Father has for His children. Draw near to Christ and you will draw near to the Father's love.

Notes

1. Warren Wiersbe, *The Bumps Are What You Climb On: Encouragement for Difficult Days* (Grand Rapids: Baker, 2002).

2. D. Martyn Lloyd-Jones, *Romans—Final Perseverance of the Saints—Exposition of the Chapter 8:17–39* (Grand Rapids: Zondervan, 1975), 339.

3. George Matheson, "O Love that Wilt Not Let Me Go," 1882.

PERSONAL QUESTIONS

1. Describe a time in your life when you doubted God's love for you.

   a. What caused this time of doubt?

   b. How did you overcome this doubt?

2. Read Romans 8:35-39.

   a. What situations does Paul list in verse 35 that some might think would cause them to be separated from God's love?

   b. Why can Paul confidently say that those situations will not separate a person from God's love?

c. Read 2 Corinthians 11:26. What types of peril did Paul endure for the sake of the Gospel?

d. According to verse 37, why are we "more than conquerors"?

e. How does knowing that nothing can separate you from God's love give you courage in the face of difficulty?

f. List and describe the five experiences that cannot separate us from God's love that are mentioned in verses 38-39.

   •

   •

   •

•

•

g. How do these five experiences encapsulate any experience you might encounter?

h. In Whom is your confidence found? Where is it not found?

3. Read 2 Timothy 2:13. What does this verse teach you about your relationship with God? How does this truth encourage and strengthen you in your daily life?

4. What practical steps can you take to prepare yourself for a time when you might question God's love for you? Which of these steps can you take this week?

GROUP QUESTIONS

1. If comfortable, share with the group a time in your life when you doubted God's love for you, and explain how you overcame this doubt.

2. Read Romans 8:35-39 as a group.

   a. List the seven situations Paul mentions in verse 35.

   •

   •

   •

   •

   •

   •

   •

The apostle Paul gives evidence of his Hebrew background when he lists the realities in Romans 8:38-39. He lists four pairs of words, three of which are basically opposites: death/life, present/future, height/depth. When the Hebrews used pairs of words that are opposites as illustrations, they were employing a figure of speech we call today a *merism*. Merism employs pairs of opposites to represent two extremes and everything in between. Other examples of merism are found in the famous verses in Psalm 139: heaven/hell (verse 8); east/west (verse 9); darkness/light (verse 12). Paul uses merism here to emphasize that nothing can separate us from the love of God in Christ.

COURAGE WHEN FRUSTRATION DISTRESSES YOU

2 Corinthians 12:7-10

In this lesson we learn to be strong even when we're weak.

OUTLINE

The Kingdom of God is full of paradoxes: We get by giving, we live by dying, and we find strength in weakness. Avoiding pain is part of the culture we live in. Embracing pain is seen as masochistic if not foolish. But God says it is in our weakness that we find true strength in Him.

I. **The Reality of Difficulty in the Believer's Life**
   A. The Purpose of It
   B. The Pain of It

II. **The Reason for Denial in the Believer's Life**
   A. The Display of His Grace
   B. The Demonstration of His Power

III. **The Result of Discipline in the Believer's Life**
   A. He Discovers the Power in Christ
   B. He Discovers the Pleasure in Infirmities

IV. **The Remarkable Discovery of the Believer's Life**

If you are a golf fan, you no doubt remember that in the 1996 Masters Golf Tournament, Greg Norman had one of the most devastating experiences an athlete of any sport could ever suffer. After the first three rounds of the tournament, he had a virtually insurmountable six-stroke lead. Eighteen more holes of just average golf and he would win the Masters and get his coveted green jacket. But the bottom fell out for Greg Norman. On the fourth and final day of the tournament, he shot a 78; and Nick Faldo shot 67 to come from six behind and win by five strokes. It was an awful moment for the world-famous Greg Norman. But a few weeks later, in *The New York Times*, a writer by the name of Larry Dorman wrote a follow-up story about Norman's response to his devastating loss:

> After the debacle, the golf star says he experienced "the most touching few days" of his life. People from all over the world contacted him with words of encouragement. The mail ran four times the volume of what Norman received when he won the British Open in 1993. "It's changed my total outlook on life and on people," Norman says of last April's defeat. "There's no need for me to be cynical anymore. My wife said to me, 'You know, maybe this is better than winning the green jacket. Maybe now you understand the importance of it all.' I never thought I could reach out and touch people like that. And the extraordinary thing is that I did it by losing." When we are weak, some of the most beautiful things in life can happen to us.[1]

The Masters Golf Tournament is a long way from the experience of the apostle Paul in first century Macedonia when he wrote Second Corinthians. But the same principles apply: What should be our response when the frustrations of life leave us distressed and confused? How do we find courage to go on? It is not a question of "if" we will have those experiences, but "when." Therefore, we need to be prepared by studying Paul's perspective on the difficulties in his life.

THE REALITY OF DIFFICULTY IN THE BELIEVER'S LIFE

Job said, "Man is born to trouble" (Job 5:7), a reality with which Paul would definitely agree.

The Purpose of It

Sometimes the specific purpose of our difficulties is not clear, but in Paul's case, he knew exactly why he was suffering: because he had been allowed special privileges that might otherwise have led to pride on his part.

In the verses preceding 2 Corinthians 12:7, Paul tells about visiting heaven—visiting heaven! He does not reveal specifics about that visit—he even refers to himself in the third person: "I know a man" (verse 2). Fourteen years prior to his writing this epistle, he had been caught up "to the third heaven" (verse 2). Whether physically or spiritually, he did not know. But, in some state of being, he was allowed to glimpse the glory of heaven. Such an experience could easily have been Paul's downfall had he allowed it to become a means of self-promotion (as some in our day might do). Twice in this passage, Paul says he was given a condition of suffering lest he exalt himself "above measure" (verse 7).

So that Paul would not be ruined by his heavenly experience, God allowed Satan to send a "thorn" into Paul's life, something to keep him grounded in reality after what must have seemed like an unreal experience.

So, from Paul's experience, we learn that God might use a humbling situation to keep us from exalting ourselves after receiving a blessing from God.

The Pain of It

Paul's experience with difficulty was painful—the equivalent of a thorn in his flesh. Paul described the thorn as a "messenger of Satan" sent to buffet him. (*Buffet* means to "beat up on.") This situation is very much like Job's—Satan was the instrument of affliction, but he acted only with God's permission (Job 1–2).

What was Paul's "thorn in the flesh"? The Greek word for "thorn" literally means a "stake"—Paul had a figurative stake driven into his body. This is another indication of the fact that this was painful, whatever it was. So painful, in fact, that Paul asked God three times to remove it (verse 8) which God refused to do. God determines when the difficulties begin and when they end.

Some have suggested that Paul's thorn was the gradual loss of his eyesight based on a statement he made in Galatians 6:11 about writing with "large letters" at the end of that epistle. He also wrote to the Galatians that he knew they would be willing to give him their own eyes had such been possible (Galatians 4:14-15).

Archaeologist and biblical historian Sir William Ramsey believed Paul suffered from malaria. Other theories about the nature of Paul's thorn include gallstones, gout, rheumatism, sciatica, gastritis, leprosy, head lice, deafness, dental infections, and remorse over his persecution of the Church before he was saved. There is no biblical proof for any of these ideas.

I believe God left the nature of Paul's affliction unspecified for a reason: If we knew specifically what his malady was, many would have limited the application of the passage only to those who suffered with the same "thorn" as Paul. Biblical commentator Philip E. Hughes has written:

> Let us suppose that Paul had supplied specific details regarding his "thorn in the flesh," and that, for the sake of argument, it was some particular form of epilepsy; then subsequent generations of Christians, the great majority of whom have been free from this complaint, would have been inclined to dismiss the apostle's problem as one remote from the reality of their own experience.[2]

By leaving it unspecified, the principle that God's grace is sufficient in times of suffering is applicable to all who suffer. Therefore, it really doesn't matter what Paul's "thorn" was. Instead of removing Paul's thorn, He taught him to live in the power and light of the grace of God—the same thing He wants us to learn when we suffer.

THE REASON FOR DENIAL IN THE BELIEVER'S LIFE

Paul's suffering was real and it was also reasonable. "Reasonable" means there was a reason for it that justified the discomfort it brought. God always has a purpose for what He causes to happen.

The Display of His Grace

Why did God not answer Paul's request to take his thorn away? First, it was an opportunity for Paul, the apostle of God's grace, to experience God's grace firsthand: "I pleaded with the Lord three times that it might depart from me. And He said to me, 'My grace is sufficient for you'" (verses 8-9).

Getting the grace to endure pain would probably not be our first choice, would it? We would much prefer to have the pain

removed. And being human, perhaps Paul felt that way at first. After all, he kept asking God—three times! But how will we ever learn that God's grace is sufficient if we don't experience that grace?

The great preacher, Charles Haddon Spurgeon, after speaking to his ministerial students which he did every week, said to them at the end of a particular lesson: "There are many passages of Scripture which you will never understand until some trying experience shall interpret them to you. The other evening I was riding home after a heavy day's work. I was wearied and depressed; and swiftly and suddenly as a lightning flash, this text laid hold on me: My grace is sufficient for you! When I got home, I looked it up in the original, and finally it dawned upon me what the text was saying, MY grace is sufficient for THEE."

"'Why,' I said to myself, 'I should think it is!' and I burst out laughing. It seemed to make unbelief so absurd. It was as though some little fish, being very thirsty, was troubled about drinking the river dry; and Father River said; 'Drink away, little fish, my stream is sufficient for you!' Or as if a little mouse in the granaries of Egypt, after seven years of plenty, feared lest it should die of famine, and Joseph said, 'Cheer up, little mouse, my granaries are sufficient for you!' Again I imagined a man way up on the mountain saying to himself, 'I fear I shall exhaust all the oxygen in the atmosphere.' But the earth cries, 'Breathe away, O man, and fill your lungs; my atmosphere is sufficient for you!'"

Spurgeon learned that the supply of God's grace is inexhaustible; it is more than sufficient "for thee"! And therein is the lesson—the reason: When you think God is not answering you, He may just be trying to show you that His grace is sufficient for you if you will only appropriate it and walk in it.

My mother was a collector of the poetry of Annie Johnson Flint. One of her most famous poems fits our subject perfectly:

God hath not promised
Skies always blue,
Flower-strewn pathways;
All our lives through;
God hath not promised
Sun without rain,
Joy without sorrow,
Peace without pain,

But God hath promised
Strength for the day
Rest for the labor,
Light for the way
Grace for all trials,
Help from above,
Unfailing sympathy,
Undying love.

It is worth going through the defining moments in life when you realize you have no resource but God alone . . . in order to learn that you need no resource but God alone! God is enough! Whatever your need, His grace is sufficient "for thee."

The Demonstration of His Power

But there was a second reason why Paul was denied relief from his thorn in the flesh: so God could demonstrate His power. The only way Paul would come to know God's power was by seeing his own human weakness. We live so much of our lives in our own strength that sometimes God has to take that strength away in order for us to see the difference between our strength and His.

A. B. Simpson, a well known missionary leader and devotional writer, said it this way:

Here is the secret of Divine all-sufficiency, to come to the end of everything in ourselves and in our circumstances. When we reach this place, we will stop asking for sympathy because of our hard situation or bad treatment, for we will recognize these things as the very conditions of our blessing, and we will turn from them to God and find in them a claim upon Him.

Our problems become the bumps that we climb on toward God.

THE RESULT OF DISCIPLINE IN THE BELIEVER'S LIFE

There is reality in the difficulties of life, and there are reasons why God sometimes denies our requests during those difficulties. But there are also results from the discipline God exercises toward us.

He Discovers the Power in Christ

There is power in Christ that we must discover, and the only way we can discover it is to be in a position of weakness: "Therefore most

gladly I will rather boast in my infirmities, that the power of Christ may rest upon me" (verse 9).

Here's a summary of what Paul learned in his situation of weakness:

You will not be without the grace to do your job. You will not be without strength to be My ambassador. But the creative difference will be this: Your weakness will serve to magnify the glory of God's power in such a way that no one will ever again be able to explain you in human terms.

Sometimes God removes all the props from under our life so we are required to depend totally on Him. It's in that stripped-down mode that we sometimes get our first glimpse of who we are and who we can become in Christ. When I was a young pastor just starting out in ministry, someone gave me a quote I've never forgotten: "God will never greatly use a person until He crushes him." And I remember specifically praying that I could be the exception! I said, "Lord, isn't there some way you can use me without that?" I wasn't the exception, and neither will you be. Nobody ever gets used mightily of God unless they experience the crucible that Paul is talking about in this passage of Scripture.

And don't think you can just decide not to be used in order to avoid suffering. God saved you for works that He has planned for you (Ephesians 2:10). To run the other way is to miss the majesty and miracle of what it means to be a Christian.

And if you're eager to be used by God, you don't have to pray for problems: "Lord, send me a thorn so I can be more effective." You just start serving Christ and let God worry about the refinement. He will handle that in His own way and time. When it comes, just yield to what God is doing. Ask Him to show you what He wants you to learn through the experience so you can become a better servant for Him.

He Discovers the Pleasure in Infirmities

It sounds strange, even morbid to a degree, to say that one takes pleasure in infirmities, but that's what Paul said: "Therefore I take pleasure in infirmities" (verse 10). It's not pain that Paul took pleasure in—he was not a sadist or a masochist. He took pleasure in knowing that God was at work in his life; that he was going to learn to experience God's grace more deeply through his "infirmities . . . reproaches . . . needs . . . persecutions . . . [and] distresses" (verse 10).

George Matheson, the blind Scottish preacher, said about the value of the thorn in his life:

> My God, I have never thanked You for my thorn. I have thanked You a thousand times for my roses, but not once for my thorn. I have been looking forward to a world where I shall get compensation for my cross; but I have never thought of my cross as itself a present glory. Teach me the glory of my cross; teach me the value of my thorn. Show me that I have climbed to You by the path of pain. Show me that my tears have made my rainbows.[3]

Our culture is based on the idea of removing as much pain as we can from life, getting rid of all the inconvenience. One of the goals of technology and medicine and new products is to make life easier, to lessen the pain. And that's fine in many regards. The problem is that we carry over that pain-free mentality to the spiritual life and are surprised—even frustrated and mad—when God decides to allow us to experience discomfort or pain.

It is counter-cultural to embrace pain; we want to turn it off as quickly as possible. But God wants us to embrace everything that comes from Him and discern why He has allowed it. What does He want us to learn from the situation we're in? He wants us to have the attitude that, without the pain we're experiencing, there is something we would never otherwise learn.

Ron Mehl was a deeply spiritual friend who lived for years with a serious form of cancer. When he finally died, he had lived longer than anyone else had with that particular disease. Here is what he wrote about what he learned:

> Storms always leave us with a list of things to clean up and fix. They are times when God restores to us the things we lose through negligence, ignorance, rebellion, or sin. For the Christian, storms are a no-lose proposition. They help us to see and acknowledge the loose shutters, missing shingles, and rotten fence posts in my life while turning me back to the only One who can make the necessary repairs.[4]

Storms wash away the dirt and debris; they have a purifying effect on the environment. And so they help to clean up our lives as well. And the question is not whether we will have storms or

not—I haven't met anyone in this life who doesn't experience them. The question is, What is our attitude going to be about them when they come? It took time even for someone as spiritual as Paul to see the value of what God was doing. Remember, he prayed three times that God would take his pain away. But three times God answered Paul with, "My grace is sufficient for you" (verse 9). He told Paul that He had something far better, far more exciting, for Paul than a pain-free life: a grace-filled life. And that is what He promises us today. Thankfully, we can learn from Paul's experience and be prepared to receive God's grace when troubles come.

THE REMARKABLE DISCOVERY OF THE BELIEVER'S LIFE

Paul's summary statement of what he learned through wrestling with his thorn is, "For when I am weak, then I am strong" (verse 10). That's not double-talk. He means that when he is weak in himself, he is strong in Christ, strong in the grace of God.

There have been times in my life when I have had responsibilities I didn't see how I could accomplish. I felt weak, or sick, or powerless. And I have learned to go to the Lord in prayer and simply say, "Lord, I can't do this. I am powerless in my own strength to accomplish what You have set before me. I am weak, Lord, but I know You are strong. I ask You to break through in my life and give me sufficient grace to meet the challenges ahead." And He always does. Things always seem to go better when I am at my human weakest and God is at His divine strongest.

However, sometimes we like to take credit for what God has done, like the woodpecker that was pecking on a tree right when a bolt of lightning split it down the middle. When we do that, God shuts off the lightning. "God resists the proud, but gives grace to the humble" (James 4:6).

Lest we ever think we are too good to have to learn God's grace this way, remember that God's own Son learned obedience through the things He suffered (Hebrews 5:8). He also learned to yield His own will to the will of His Father (Luke 22:42-44). Matthew records that Jesus prayed, submitting His will to God's will, three different times (Matthew 26:43-44).

If Paul and Jesus Christ learned to appropriate the grace of God in times of great "frustration," you and I can too. Instead of praying for God to take your trouble away, pray that He would give you more grace.

Notes

1. Larry Dorman, "Support from Around the World Overwhelms Norman," *The New York Times*, April 18, 1996, sec. B, 11, as seen in *Reader's Digest*, September 1996, 106.

2. Philip E. Hughes, *The New International Commentary on the New Testament, The Second Epistle to the Corinthians* (Grand Rapids: Eerdmans Publishing, 1962), 442.

3. *Streams in the Desert* (Zondervan Publishing Company, 1997), 109.

4. Ron Mehl, *Surprise Endings* (Oregon: Multnomah Press, 1993), 60.

1. Read 2 Corinthians 12:7-10.

   a. Why was Paul suffering from a "thorn in the flesh"? (See 2 Corinthians 12:1-5.)

   b. What might Paul's "thorn" have been? (See Galatians 4:14-15; 6:11.)

   c. Have you experienced a difficulty ("thorn in the flesh") like Paul's? If so, what was it?

   d. How many times did Paul ask God to remove his "thorn"? (verse 8)

e. What was God's answer to him? (verse 9)

f. In what way(s) have you seen God's grace be sufficient for you when you've encountered prolonged suffering in your life?

g. What is one way God has used a difficulty to refine you and make you more like Him?

h. Explain why it is worth learning that God is enough, even when the lesson comes by way of a trial.

f. Why didn't God answer Paul's request for Him to remove this "thorn" from his life? (verse 9)

g. How do we come to know God's power in our life?

h. What should our response be when God brings trials and difficulties into our life?

i. If comfortable, share with the group a time when God used a trial to refine you.

j. Discuss why it is counter-cultural to embrace pain.

k. Why does God want us to embrace pain?

2. Read Luke 22:42-44 and Matthew 26:43-44 together.

a. What do these verses teach us about Jesus and His submission to the Father?

b. How is Jesus an example to us in the area of submitting to pain and suffering?

DID YOU KNOW?

Paul equates the "third heaven" which he visited with "Paradise" (2 Corinthians 12:2, 4). The Greek word for Paradise is *paradeisos*, which means literally a "park." It is found only two other times in the New Testament: when Jesus told the thief on the cross he would be with Jesus in Paradise (Luke 23:43) and as the location of the "tree of life" (Revelation 2:7). The Greek version of the Old Testament (the Septuagint) used the word to describe Eden (Genesis 2:15; 3:23) and the lush plains of the Jordan River valley in which Lot chose to dwell (Genesis 13:10).

COURAGE WHEN FOES DEMORALIZE YOU

Daniel 3:16-30

In this lesson we learn what it means to take a stand for God in the face of opposition.

OUTLINE

Everyone is committed to defending something—a sports team, a political persuasion, or a moral issue. But how many people would defend their favorite issue to the death? It takes courage to stand firm when the world is gathered against you. And courage comes from belief in God.

I. The Record of Their Deliverance
  A. The King's Anger
  B. The King's Action
  C. The King's Astonishment
  D. The King's Acknowledgement
  E. The King's Announcement

II. The Reasons for Their Deliverance
  A. They Had an Absolute Commitment to God
  B. They Had Absolute Confidence in God
  C. They Had Absolute Courage for God
  D. They Had Absolute Consciousness of God

III. The Result of Their Deliverance
  A. Their Enemies Were Executed
  B. Their Bonds Were Eliminated
  C. Their Hearts Were Encouraged
  D. Their God Was Exalted
  E. Their Influence Was Enlarged

OVERVIEW

Out of the fall of Communism in eastern Europe came knowledge of a great leader of the church in Romania named Joseph Tson. While Romania was still Communist-controlled, he was arrested by the secret police for publishing a sermon calling for the churches to refuse to submit to the Communist government's demand for control over their ministries. When a Communist official told him that he had to renounce his sermon, he replied, "No, sir, I won't do that."

The official, surprised that anyone would respond so forcefully to the secret police, said, "Aren't you aware that I can use force against you?"

"Sir," said Joseph Tson, "let me explain how this works. You see, your supreme weapon is killing, and my supreme weapon is dying. You know that my sermons are spread all over the country on tapes. When you kill me, I only sprinkle them with my blood. They will speak ten times louder after that because everybody will say, 'That preacher meant it, because he sealed it with his blood.' So go on, sir. Kill me. When you kill me, I win the supreme victory."

And the secret police released him, knowing that his martyrdom would be far more of a problem than his sermon was.

The courage of Joseph Tson is reminiscent of three men who lived in another time in another place: Shadrach, Meshach, and Abed-Nego. They lived in Babylon two-and-a-half millennia ago, and their story is recorded in Daniel chapter 3. Their courage has strengthened millions of believers over the centuries, and it will strengthen ours today.

These three young Hebrew men were taken with Daniel as captives from Jerusalem to Babylon. We read in the first part of chapter 3 that the king of Babylon, a megalomaniac named Nebuchadnezzar, had set up a huge gold image of himself that was to be worshiped by all the people of Babylon—including the captive Hebrews. The statue was ninety feet tall and nine feet wide—tall and thin—and it towered over everything else around.

The purpose of the image was to unify the nation of Babylon around himself. Because Babylon was polytheistic in their view of the cosmos—they worshiped many gods—Nebuchadnezzar's plan was to use the image to unite the worship of the people around himself. In that sense, he was setting himself forth to be a god— he was deifying himself in the eyes of his people.

When the image was complete, word went out that all the people were to come and fall down and worship the image when the signal was given (Daniel 3:4-6). Some scholars have estimated that as many as three hundred thousand people would have been summoned to worship the image. When the musical signal was given, all the people came to the plain of Dura and fell down prostrate before the image of Nebuchadnezzar. All, that is, except for three: Shadrach, Meshach, and Abed-Nego. They probably stood out as plainly as did Nebuchadnezzar's tall, skinny statue. They were the only ones left standing when everyone else was on their faces in front of the statue.

The reason the three Hebrew men didn't worship the statue is that it would have been a violation of Exodus 20:4-5 (the second of the Ten Commandments): "You shall not make for yourself a carved image—any likeness of anything that is in heaven above, or that is in the earth beneath, or that is in the water under the earth; you shall not bow down to them nor serve them."

Nebuchadnezzar appears to have been willing to give the three men a second chance (Daniel 3:13-15). He finishes his ultimatum by saying they would be cast into a "burning fiery furnace" if they did not fall down and worship: "And who is the god who will deliver you from my hands?" (verse 15)

The three Hebrew men did not ask for a minute to get their thoughts together or decide how to react to the king's ultimatum. They knew exactly what their answer was, just like Joseph Tson, the Romanian pastor.

Shadrach, Meshach, and Abed-Nego answered and said to the king, "O Nebuchadnezzar, we have no need to answer you in this matter. If that is the case, our God whom we serve is able to deliver us from the burning fiery furnace, and He will deliver us from your hand, O king. But if not, let it be known to you, O king, that we do not serve your gods, nor will we worship the gold image which you have set up" (verses 16-18).

When I read their words, it makes me want to stand up and shout, "Where are the believers like that today?" They knew exactly what they believed and where the line was that they were not willing to cross—not even for a king who had the power to put them to death. They were okay with the fact that God might not rescue them: "If He does, okay; if He doesn't, that's okay too." Life on earth was not as important to them as remaining obedient and faithful to God.

We need people like Shadrach, Meshach, and Abed-Nego today—and that is the heart of this lesson: how to maintain courage even when your enemies are trying to demoralize you.

THE RECORD OF THEIR DELIVERANCE

First, let's look at the basic facts of their story.

The King's Anger

Nebuchadnezzar had an angry temperament. I guess if you're used to ruling with an iron fist, that's not surprising. Verse 19 suggests that his facial expression became distorted and changed when the three Hebrew men responded to him about not worshiping his idol. He was not used to having people talk back to him and disobey his order.

The King's Action

Nebuchadnezzar allowed his rage to take control, and he made good on his threat—he threw the three Hebrew men into the fiery furnace. It had been heated so hot that it killed the Babylonian guards who took the three to the furnace!

The King's Astonishment

When the king went to check on the status of the punishment, he was amazed to find not three, but four men walking around in the furnace. And strangely enough, the fourth man had an appearance "like the Son of God" (verse 25).

The King's Acknowledgement

When Nebuchadnezzar had the three Hebrews removed from the furnace, he acknowledged that their God had sent His Angel to deliver the three men. He acknowledged that the reason they were rescued was that they "yielded their bodies, that they should not serve nor worship any god except their own God!" (verse 28)

The King's Announcement

Nebuchadnezzar knows a winning team when he sees one, so he issues a new decree to all the people in Babylon: Anybody who says anything bad about the God of Shadrach, Meshach, and Abed-Nego will be put to death.

THE REASONS FOR THEIR DELIVERANCE

The courage these young men demonstrated was not accidental. There are reasons why they were strong; and we can incorporate those same reasons into our lives, mirroring their strength when we find ourselves in our own "fiery furnace."

They Had an Absolute Commitment to God

In verse 18, the three Hebrew men took an unequivocal stand: "We do not serve your gods, nor will we worship the gold image which you have set up."

I believe the secret to success in the Christian life has been, and always will be, obedience to God and His Word. In the case of the three Hebrew men, they knew the Ten Commandments—that was the part of God's Word to which they were committed and on which they took their stand. They weren't interested in dialogue or negotiation. They knew what they believed and were not going to waver.

Are you and I committed to God at that same level of obedience? We read the polls about how many Americans profess to be Christians, but fail to see the evidence in the moral fabric of society. It may be that Dr. Howard Hendricks' observation is true: "The evangelical movement is 40 miles wide and an eighth of an inch deep." If our commitment to God and His Word is no deeper than that, we will not stand firm when the fire heats up.

One of the Early Church fathers named Athanasius was a champion for the doctrine of the deity of Jesus Christ and engaged in many theological battles defending that doctrine. Someone came to him once and said, "Athanasius, the emperor is against you, the bishops are against you, and the church is against you. In fact, the whole world is against you, Athanasius."

And Athanasius said, "Then I am against the whole world." His words became a watchword for faithfulness during that part of Church history. If that's what it takes, we must be prepared to stand against the whole world in our commitment to God.

They Had Absolute Confidence in God

Note the four small words that give evidence of the men's confidence in God: "Our God . . . is able" (verse 17). God is able! That's all we need to know when we find ourselves attacked by the enemies of God. God is in control; God is able to do whatever He chooses in our situation. The men didn't say, "God will deliver us." They said, "God is able." The difference is significant. They were willing to trust God for whatever He decided to do. They didn't make their confidence contingent upon being delivered. Their confidence was based on the character of God, not what He chose to do at that moment.

They Had Absolute Courage for God

The Hebrew men did not express their commitment and confidence in God out of a sense of macho bravado. They did it out of courage! They knew Nebuchadnezzar and his reputation for cruelty. He was one of the cruelest tyrants in the history of ancient civilizations, willing to dispose of human life without a thought. When Shadrach, Meshach, and Abed-Nego said, "We do not serve your gods, nor will we worship the gold image" (verse 18), they knew that their very lives were at stake.

When Martin Luther was on his way to be excommunicated from the church and to appear before King Charles V and the Roman Prelate and all the assembled princes, this is what he said:

My cause shall be commended to the Lord, for He lives and reigns, who preserved the three Hebrew children in the furnace of the Babylonian king. If He is unwilling to preserve me, my life is a small thing compared with Christ. Expect anything of me except flight or recantation. I will not flee much less recant, so may the Lord Jesus strengthen me.

Proverbs 29:25 says it this way: "The fear of man brings a snare, but whoever trusts in the Lord shall be safe."

They Had Absolute Consciousness of God

When Nebuchadnezzar looked into the fiery furnace and saw a fourth figure, he recognized that the figure was divine. He wouldn't have known what the true Son of God looked like, of course. What he saw looked like a son of the gods to him. But we know it was the Lord Jesus Christ Himself, communing with the three brave Hebrew men.

God promises to be with us when we "walk through the fire" (Isaiah 43:2). "When you walk through the fire, you shall not be burned, nor shall the flame scorch you." That promise of God through Isaiah was fulfilled directly in the lives of the three Hebrew men. God is with us in whatever circumstance we find ourselves: sickness, divorce, financial struggles, job loss—it doesn't matter. He promises to be with us and not let the "flames" destroy us.

I've said this to my congregation before—and I say it carefully to them, and to you now, lest I be misunderstood: It's almost worth going into the fire to experience the presence of God with us.

THE RESULT OF THEIR DELIVERANCE

We've looked at the reality of what happened and the reasons why the Hebrew men acted as they did, but the most important part is the result of their deliverance. What happens when we exercise courage in the face of opposition?

Their Enemies Were Executed

The men who obeyed the king's orders to throw Shadrach, Meshach, and Abed-Nego into the furnace were themselves killed by the heat of the fire (verse 22).

The ancient furnaces were capable of reaching incredible temperatures. They were large, domed structures with vents on the top and bellows beneath for pumping air into the furnace and heating it to high temperatures. There would have been some sort of door or entryway for inserting the metal or bricks or whatever was to be heated in the furnace, and when this door was opened, the Hebrew men fell into the furnace; but the Babylonians were consumed by the heat.

In one fell swoop, those who attacked the children of God were consumed; and the children of God were preserved. That doesn't mean that Christians are always going to be protected from every dangerous threat—we know from experience that isn't true. But we do know that often something we thought was going to be truly horrific turns out not to have been so bad at all because God was with us in the midst of it. When we exercise courage because of our commitment to and confidence in God, He shows up to make a difference.

Their Bonds Were Eliminated

Verse 21 tells us that when the Hebrew men were thrown into the furnace, they were bound hand and foot. But when Nebuchadnezzar looked into the furnace, he saw the three men (plus the Son of God) walking around in the furnace, no longer bound (verse 25). All that got burned up in this fire were the Babylonian guards and the Babylonian rope that was used to bind the three Hebrew men.

It's an interesting reminder to us that sometimes God puts us in the fire so He can purge from us the things that are holding us back and holding us down and keeping us from walking free in the will of God.

Their Hearts Were Encouraged

When Nebuchadnezzar looked inside the furnace, what he saw was a Christophany—an Old Testament appearance of the eternal Son of God, Jesus Christ. Christ is eternal. He did not begin to exist when He was born at Bethlehem. Instead, He was incarnated in fleshly form at Bethlehem. He came to earth in the form and likeness of mankind in order that He might announce to men the coming of the Kingdom of God and ultimately die in the place of men for their sins. Therefore, what Nebuchadnezzar saw in the fiery furnace was a preincarnate image of Jesus Christ—a Christophany.

Sometimes the very trials we resist and even resent are the very means by which God wants to reveal Himself to us in a personal way. You may be in a fiery furnace of some sort as you are reading this lesson. You need to know that God is with you—that He has promised never to leave you nor forsake you (Hebrews 13:5). Even if you think you are alone, you are not. Even if you don't understand, God does. All you need do is draw near to God, and He will draw near to you (James 4:8). He will carry you through and comfort you through the situation you are in.

Please note: God did not rescue the three Hebrew men *from* the fiery furnace. He rescued them *in* the fiery furnace. God has not promised there won't be any fires, as much as we would like Him to. Some people are shocked when they become Christians that there are still fiery furnaces to go through. That's the norm—we are going to have trials and tribulations as believers because we are now moving against the current of this world. But the difference is that we don't go through those trials alone—we go through them in the presence of God.

The second verse of one of the great hymns of the faith, "How Firm a Foundation," says it best:

When through fiery trials
Thy pathways shall lie
My grace, all sufficient
Shall be thy supply
The flame shall not hurt thee
I only design
Thy dross to consume
And thy gold to refine.

Their God Was Exalted

As a result of God's miraculous preservation of the Hebrew men, Nebuchadnezzar declared that the God of the Hebrews should be defended in Babylon. Anyone who spoke ill of or against the God of the Hebrews would be "cut in pieces, and their houses . . . made an ash heap" (verse 29).

In the ancient world, the god with the most power became the prominent god. Life consisted of one power encounter after another. And the God of the Hebrews was immediately elevated to the top tier of the Babylonian pantheon because of what He did in preserving the Hebrew men. This was a radical turnaround for Nebuchadnezzar. At the beginning of this story, he was full of himself. Now he is full of awareness of the power of the God of the Hebrews.

And that will happen today. God will be exalted in our midst when we display the same kind of courage that the Hebrew men displayed. People will see the results of His presence and power and lift Him up just as Nebuchadnezzar did.

Their Influence Was Enlarged

At the end of the day, "the king promoted Shadrach, Meshach, and Abed-Nego in the province of Babylon" (verse 30). That was an unexpected end to an unplanned day for some unlikely heroes of the faith. They started out being arrested and thrown into a furnace and ended up being promoted to positions of prominence in Nebuchadnezzar's kingdom. That is something only God could have accomplished for these three. I believe God takes great delight in confounding the world that way—doing exactly the opposite of what the world thinks should have happened.

Chrysostom was one of the greatest of the Early Church fathers (A.D. 347–407). As a very young Christian, he was brought before the emperor. The emperor said to him that if he would not give up Christ, but insisted on becoming a Christian, "I will banish you from your country and from your father's land."

Chrysostom said, "You cannot banish me. The whole world is my Father's land."

Well, the emperor then said, "I will take away all your property."

Chrysostom said, "You cannot. My treasures are in heaven."

So the emperor said, "I will take you to a place where there is not a friend to speak to you."

Chrysostom replied, "You cannot do that. I have a friend who sticks closer to me than a brother. I shall have my brother, Jesus Christ, forever."

And the emperor finally threatened, "I will take away your life."

And Chrysostom replied, "You cannot take away my life, because my life is hid with God in Christ."

And the emperor left him alone. What do you do with a man who is not threatened by anything?

Nebuchadnezzar could not threaten Shadrach, Meshach, and Abed-Nego. You don't have to be discouraged when your foes attempt to demoralize you, either. You just have to know what you believe and in whom you believe.

1. Read Daniel 3.

   a. What did King Nebuchadnezzar make? (verse 1)

   b. Why did he make this image?

   c. What did King Nebuchadnezzar command all the people to do once the image was completed? (verses 4-5)

   d. Why didn't Shadrach, Meshach, and Abed-Nego bow down to the image?

   e. What was their punishment for refusing to bow down to the image? (verses 6, 15)

f. In verse 15, what question does King Nebuchadnezzar ask the three men?

g. What is their answer to the king's question? (verses 16-18)

h. What phrase indicates that the three men were confident in God? (verse 17)

i. On what was their confidence based?

j. What happened to the men who threw Shadrach, Meshach, and Abed-Nego into the fiery furnace? (verse 22)

k. How did the furnace affect the three Hebrew men? (verses 25, 27)

l. What was the unexpected ending for the three men? (verse 30)

2. Explain how God used this situation to bring glory to Himself.

3. Read Proverbs 29:25. How might this verse give you strength when you are faced with the choice to obey God or to obey man?

4. Has there been a time in your life when you took a stand for the truth of God's Word and no one else around you did? If so, describe how God gave you courage during that moment and explain how He used it for His glory.

1. Read Daniel 3 as a group.

   a. Describe what happened in this chapter.

   b. Who were the main characters?

   c. What was the conflict that occurred?

   d. What stand did the three Hebrew men take?

   e. What were the consequences of their courageous actions?

   f. How did God rescue the three men?

g. Share with the group any details or aspects of this chapter that stand out to you.

2. Read Proverbs 29:25 together.

   a. What does the fear of man bring?

   b. What happens when we trust in the Lord?

   c. Share with the group how this verse can give you strength when you are faced with the choice to obey God or to obey man.

3. Think about our current culture. What type of stands will we possibly need to make for Christ in the future? How can we have courage and boldness to obey God's Word no matter the consequences? Pray for each other as a group that God would give you courage to stand for the Truth.

4. Review the "Did You Know?" section at the end of the lesson.

   a. What is the difference between a theophany and a Christophany?

   b. In addition to the fourth Man appearing in the fiery furnace in Daniel 3, what are some other theophanies found in the Old Testament? (See Genesis 3:8; 18:1; Exodus 22:22-35.)

DID YOU KNOW?

The appearance of the Son of God in the furnace with the three Hebrew men was, generally speaking, a theophany (an appearance of God), and specifically a Christophany (an appearance of Christ). There is reason to believe that all appearances of God in the Old Testament were appearances of the Son of God. Theophany is a compound of two Greek words: *theos* (God), and *phainein* (to appear). Theophanies in the Old Testament took many forms: God walked in the Garden of Eden with Adam and Eve (Genesis 3:8) and appeared to Abraham at the door of his tent (Genesis 18:1). The Angel of the Lord in the Old Testament is most likely a theophany (Genesis 16:7-11; 22:1, 15; Exodus 3:2; Numbers 22:22-35).

COURAGE WHEN YOUR FUTURE DEPRESSES YOU

Joshua 1:1-9

*In this lesson we discover God's principles
for success.*

OUTLINE

There is an unknown aspect of life for every human being alive at
this moment: the future. No one knows what it holds. For that reason,
everyone is tempted to be fearful of it. Joshua faced an unknown
future until God gave him six principles of success—and promised
he would prosper.

  I. **The Principle of Divine Perspective**

 II. **The Principle of Divine Purpose**

III. **The Principle of Divine Persuasion**

IV. **The Principle of Divine Priority**
     A. Talk About It Constantly
     B. Meditate on It Continually
     C. Read It Obediently
     D. Follow It Exclusively
     E. Accept It Totally

  V. **The Principle of Divine Presence**

 VI. **The Principle of Divine Prosperity**

OVERVIEW

I believe the passage of Scripture we will study in this lesson holds the key to success in the Christian life. That makes it pretty important, I'm sure you will agree. No human can guarantee success in life, but God can! I hope you will take this passage to heart.

The context of this passage is transitions—the transition of leadership in Israel from Moses to Joshua. Moses is still revered today as one of the greatest figures in Jewish history. How would you like to have been Joshua, taking the reins of leadership from someone like Moses? Moses had led Israel out of bondage in Egypt, across the Red Sea to Mount Sinai where God gave him the Ten Commandments, and then across the wilderness to the Promised Land.

Exodus 33:11 says something about Moses that was not said about any other person in Scripture: He spoke to the Lord "face to face." Moses was on intimate terms with God. He received instructions for Israel from God and then communicated them to the people. Though the people often grumbled against Moses, they knew he was God's man. They chafed against his leadership and loved him all at the same time. When Moses died "the children of Israel wept for [him] in the plains of Moab thirty days" (Deuteronomy 34:8).

Moses' death came at a perilous time. The generation that failed to believe God at Kadesh Barnea had died off during forty years of wandering in the wilderness. Now the new generation that replaced them was gathered on the east bank of the Jordan River, ready to cross over and inherit the Promised Land. The people of Canaan, who would have to be driven out of the land, were large in stature, well organized socially and militarily, and far advanced in civilization and technologies like metallurgy for making weapons (Joshua 17:16).

The Israelites were not prepared at all to conduct military campaigns. The generation about to go into the land had been living in the wilderness for forty years, being fed a day at a time by God. In the midst of this situation, God tells Joshua he is the new leader of the nation!

If you had been called in as a consultant to help Joshua prepare for his new role, what would you have told him?

Thankfully, Joshua did have a consultant—a divine one: God Himself. God delivered to Joshua one of the most powerful motivational speeches I have ever read. This speech has helped me many times in my life, and I believe it will help you at a time when you are "stuck"—not sure that you can succeed in the task you are attempting.

In this lesson we will study God's six-point plan for success in life, originally delivered on the plains of Moab to Joshua.

THE PRINCIPLE OF DIVINE PERSPECTIVE

Notice that God mentions Moses twice in Joshua 1: in verse 3 and verse 5. The purpose of these two references is to provide historical context for Joshua, to remind him of what he had experienced as Moses' assistant and partner in ministry. It was as if God was saying to Joshua, "I was with Moses, and I will be with you!"

One of the most important things we can ever do as we face the uncertainties of the future in our life is to remember what God has done for us in the past. I read the biographies of great Christian leaders from the past for that very reason: "Lord, You did it for David Livingstone in Africa, so I know You can do it for David Jeremiah in America!"

It was time for Joshua to get over what someone has called the "second lieutenant mentality." He was no longer the number two man in Israel; he was soon to become the leader. He had to realize that God was going to be with him just as He had been with Moses.

THE PRINCIPLE OF DIVINE PURPOSE

Once Joshua had a divine perspective on his task, he was given a divine purpose: to settle the Promised Land that God had promised to Abraham for his descendants (verses 2-4). Joshua needed to stay focused. Many distractions would arise along the way—he needed never to forget the purpose of his appointment as leader of Israel.

The land was a gift to Israel, but they still had to appropriate it— to walk over all the land and claim it as their own. It was theirs, but they had to reach out and take it.

There is something very liberating and invigorating about knowing what you are supposed to do. You can get up every morning, make your "to-do" list, and go forward to accomplish your purpose. When you don't know what you're supposed to do, life gets foggy and confusing.

When our church went through a series of studies on finding your purpose in life, we lost some people from our church! They didn't leave mad—they just discovered that God's purpose for them was in another city or state, and they left. I hated to see them go, but was glad they discovered God's purpose for their lives. Purpose gives direction and energy for life.

THE PRINCIPLE OF DIVINE PERSUASION

Even with all his experience with God and Moses, Joshua needed a little prodding. So the next thing he received was divine persuasion:

- "Be strong and of good courage" (verse 6).
- "Only be strong and very courageous" (verse 7).
- "Be strong and of good courage" (verse 9).

If I had to guess, I would say God was trying to impress upon Joshua the need to be very strong and very courageous! That is the heart of God's motivational message to Joshua.

"Strong" means resolute—not easily swayed from one's purpose by the efforts of others. "Courageous" has a sense of "daring" in it; an element of risk-taking. (Think of the daring it would take to march around Jericho for a week!) Strength and courage mean the willingness to stay on point regardless of how hard the winds blow against you and be willing to obey God when the naysayers are opposing you.

Joshua displayed these traits when he and Caleb returned from scouting out the land with the other ten spies. They were the only spies who believed Israel could take the land by believing God's promises. The other ten spies were afraid of the giants in the land —they were focused on the opposition. But Joshua and Caleb were focused on God. They were in the minority, but they held their ground —even though the rest of Israel voted with the pessimistic majority.

The majority is not always right! Sometimes the minority report is the one that reflects God's will. Think about Jesus Himself—was He, and were His followers, in the majority or the minority? To be a leader requires standing strong for what you know is right and not wavering. There are millions of people in the former Soviet Union and Soviet bloc countries today who are thankful that President Ronald Reagan opposed Communism until it disintegrated. Leadership can be lonely, but it should not be abandoned just because it is.

Paul Lawrence Dunbar has reminded us in poetic form that:

Minorities, since time began,
Have shown the better side of man;
And often in the lists of time
One man has made a cause sublime.[1]

I love to read these verses in Joshua when I am facing challenges in my life. It helps me regain God's perspective on my purpose and persuades me to be firm and willing to take risks for God. That's what God was doing for Joshua, and it has the same effect on me. And I believe it will for you, as well.

THE PRINCIPLE OF DIVINE PRIORITY

Now we come to the heart of the matter: It is not possible to find success in our purposes in life unless we walk according to God's Word.

God didn't tell Joshua that his priority needed to be military strategy, financial backing, or bilateral relations with neighboring countries. Those things have a place, but they are not the priority. Here was Joshua's priority: Meditate day and night upon the principles of the Word of God. Here are five ways one goes about maintaining that priority.

Talk About It Constantly

When God says, "This Book of the Law shall not depart from your mouth" (verse 8), He is saying it is to be Joshua's constant subject of conversation. Not talking *about* the law of God like we would talk about a novel or other interesting book, but allowing the law of God to inform, guide, and temper all his conversations and deliberations. We see Joshua doing that in Joshua 8:34-35: When Joshua stood up to instruct the people, he didn't give them *his* perspective, he read them God's Book of the Law.

What if Christians, instead of talking only about politics, TV shows, movies, sports, and the traffic, started talking about the Word of God? "What did you learn from the Word today?" "Before we discuss our plans, let's talk about what the Word says about what we're about to undertake." Wouldn't that be a refreshing way to live?

If you decide to do that, be forewarned: You're going to lose some "friends." Not everybody is interested in talking about God's Word more than anything else.

Meditate on It Continually

The purpose of meditating on the Word of God is to fill your mind so full of the truth that you won't be misled or victimized by the errors of this world. It is impossible to live in our world today and not have things spilled on us that we want no part of. But that doesn't mean those things have to stain us. The Word acts like a stain-resistant coating on our heart and mind. We may hear and see things that we wish weren't there, but they don't have to become snares for us.

When I was sick with cancer, I underwent a process called electrophoresis. With an IV in one arm, blood was taken out of my body. It went through a process, then it was returned through an IV in the other arm. That's what the Word of God does—the good comes in one side and pushes the bad out the other side. Instead of thinking about the bad stuff all the time, trying to resist it, you just focus on the good of God's Word. Your mind stays centered on truth instead of trash.

Read It Obediently

A critically important phrase is repeated in both verses 7 and 8: "observe to do." God tells Joshua that he must "observe to do" everything written in the Book of the Law.

We don't use the phrase "observe to do" today—but it wouldn't hurt if we did. It means that Joshua is to read and meditate and study the Word of God *for the purpose of obeying it!* He wasn't to read it so as to just know it. He was to read it so as to do it. The Bible is not primarily history or literature. It is a book of marching orders for God's people.

Follow It Exclusively

God tells Joshua that he is not to divert onto strange paths when Israel gets into Canaan. He is to follow the Word of God and not turn "to the right hand or to the left" (verse 7). He is not to compromise or to make God's laws politically correct. He is not to use God's laws as a proof-text for his own points of view. He is to obey God's laws and nothing else. If he doesn't, he will end up in the ditch by the side of the road. All Joshua had was the five books of Moses: Genesis, Exodus, Leviticus, Numbers, and Deuteronomy. But in those books was the covenant—especially as it had been restated in Deuteronomy for the new generation—and that was all

Joshua needed to be successful in the Promised Land as long as he kept that covenant.

Accept It Totally

Joshua was not to pick and choose from the books of Moses. He was to obey "all that is written in it"(verse 8). One of the problems we have in the Church today is that people know nothing of the Old Testament. Many preachers today do not preach on the whole Word of God—they stay focused just on the New Testament. I understand why they do that—we live under the new covenant, not the old. But that doesn't mean we should ignore the Old Testament, for it is the foundation of the New Testament. It is very difficult to understand the New Testament without knowing the Old. To be successful as a Christian today, we must do what God told Joshua to do: Obey all that is written in the Word of God.

Just before Joshua died, in his final address to the people, he admonished them to do exactly what God had admonished him to do: Be courageous and obey all of God's law (Joshua 23:6). He passed on to the next generation what God had given him. The instruction God gave for kings in Israel is along the same line: Make a personal copy of the laws of God, read it all your life, and obey all of it (Deuteronomy 17:18-19). When David was near the end of his life, he gave the same instructions to his son Solomon: Be strong and keep God's commandments as written in the law of Moses (1 Kings 2:2-3).

If "the Church," meaning every individual Christian, could simply substitute dwelling on and walking in obedience to the Word of God for all the other success formulas our culture offers, we would indeed be successful in every way that really counts.

We must see ourselves today just as Joshua did when he stood on the banks of the Jordan. We must see a world in front of us into which God is sending us. If we are going to be successful, we have to be fed from the Word of God daily. There are far too many churches and Christians today who are going about all their activities in life with little regard for the Word. I don't know how they expect to succeed. Soldiers for Christ need to be armed with "the sword of the Spirit, which is the word of God" (Ephesians 6:17).

I've read enough biographies of the people who have changed the world for Christ to know that they fed themselves on the Bible.

It is said that George Mueller read through the Bible two hundred times. David Livingstone read it through four times in succession while in prison in Africa. Charles Spurgeon said, "A Bible that is falling apart usually belongs to someone who is not." If Christians today would just read through the Bible once in a year, it would revolutionize the Church. God promises that His Word will never return to Him void without accomplishing the purpose for which it was sent (Isaiah 55:10-11).

If we are going to make the Word of God the priority in our life it should be, we will have to start including it in our conversation, meditating on it, reading it with a view toward obeying what we read, following it exclusively, and accepting all of it—from cover to cover.

THE PRINCIPLE OF DIVINE PRESENCE

The fifth principle for Joshua's success in the Promised Land was the principle of God's divine presence with him. We are familiar with the verse from Hebrews that says, "I will never leave you nor forsake you" (Hebrews 13:5)—and here is one of its Old Testament roots (see also Deuteronomy 31:6, 8).

God tells Joshua, "As I was with Moses, so I will be with you. I will not leave you nor forsake you" (Joshua 1:5). And in verse 9 we have God's words, "The Lord your God is with you wherever you go."

God had done everything necessary for Joshua's success. First, He gave him perspective—a context for success. Next, He reminded him of the importance of purpose—his task in settling the land of Canaan for Israel. Third, God persuaded Joshua to be strong and courageous—stay resolute and be daring. Fourth, He reminded him to make the Word of God his priority. And now, God tells Joshua the one thing Joshua probably most wanted to hear: He wasn't going into Canaan alone! God was going to be beside Joshua from the Jordan to the Mediterranean, from Dan to Beersheba.

If you are involved in a ministry for the Lord, never think you are doing it alone. As God promised to be with Joshua, so He promises to be with you.

THE PRINCIPLE OF DIVINE PROSPERITY

Finally, God gives Joshua an overwhelming promise: "No man shall be able to stand before you all the days of your life" (verse 5).

"Wow!" Joshua must have thought. "No one, for the rest of my life, will defeat me in any of my undertakings? How could this be possible?"

"It is possible," God would reply, "because you are a man of My Word. You are a man of courage and strength. You are a man who walks obediently in all My statutes and commands. And ultimately, Joshua, you will prosper because I will never leave you nor forsake you. I will be with you in all things to ensure your success. You will never be defeated if you continue in My ways."

Here is God's promise to Joshua that if he lived his life according to God's law: "You will make your way prosperous, and then you will have good success" (verse 8). "Success" meant, in the Hebrew language, to be prudent or to act circumspectly. So, in a religious and ethical sense, it means someone who let himself and his life be guided by God. Joshua had this kind of success and prosperity. He experienced hardship, and sometimes he failed. But his way was prudent and wise and, therefore, successful.

Now, picture this with me: Joshua finds out he has this new job assignment to be the leader of Israel. He goes into the divine Consultant's office and gets the six principles of success we've reviewed in this lesson. God read them out to Joshua just like you've read them here. I think when he went into the office, he might have been a bit overwhelmed, even depressed at the thought of what lay before him. But I believe when he walked out, he was standing straight and tall and there was a spring in his step. He had gotten a transfusion of courage as a result of his meeting with the divine Counselor.

I know these principles work, dear reader, because I have made them the core principles for my own walk with God. I'm not comparing myself with Joshua, but I have tried to be his apprentice —to take what God gave him and appropriate it for my own life.

These principles have transformed my life on many occasions, given me the shot of courage I needed to push on and find the success God intended. And I believe they will do the same for you.

Note

1. Paul Lawrence Dunbar, "Right's Security," *Lyrics of Lowly Life* (Secaucus, NJ: Carol Publishing Group, 1984).

1. Read Joshua 1:1-9.

   a. Explain what is happening in this passage.

   b. How would God's mention of Moses in verses 3 and 5 have encouraged Joshua?

   c. What was the divine purpose given to Joshua? (verses 2-4)

   d. What were the boundaries of the land the Lord was giving to the children of Israel? (verse 4)

   e. What was Joshua's priority to be at this time? (verses 7-8)

f. Why should God's Word inform, guide, and temper all your conversations? How do you make sure it does this?

g. What promise did God give to Joshua in verse 5 and again in verse 9?

h. What was God's promise to Joshua if he lived according to His law? (verse 8)

i. What did "success" mean in the Hebrew language? How is that different from our definition of success?

j. Describe how this passage encourages you to take risks for God in your own life.

k. When had Joshua displayed strength and courage in the past? How might his courage in previous moments have helped him as he led the people into the Promised Land?

2. Why is it important to study and understand the Old Testament and the New Testament?

a. In what ways do Christians today pick and chose what they want to obey from God's Word?

b. Why is this dangerous?

c. How can you make sure you study all of God's Word, and not just the portions you like or that are easier to understand?

GROUP QUESTIONS

1. Read Joshua 1:1-9 as a group.

   a. What is Joshua chosen to do after Moses' death? (verses 1-2)

   b. Why was it important for Joshua to remember that God had been with Moses? (verse 5)

   c. Discuss what the words *strong* and *courageous* mean.

   d. What phrase is repeated in verses 6, 7, and 9?

e. Why was it important for Joshua to be "strong and very courageous" (verse 7) as he led the children of Israel into the Promised Land?

f. In verse 8 God tells Joshua to, "Meditate in [the Book of the Law] day and night." What is the purpose of mediating on God's Word? Discuss what meditating on God's Word looks like. Why is this an important discipline for all Christians?

2. Review the six principles of success found in this lesson.

a. Why is it important to have a divine perspective as we face the uncertainties of life?

b. How does having a divine purpose provide us with clarity in our life?

c. If comfortable, share with the group about a time when you needed to be strong and courageous in the face of difficulty.

d. How do you keep God's Word as a priority in your life?

e. How does knowing that God is with us, give us courage in the midst of challenges?

f. Discuss the Hebrew definition of "success" and how it differs from our current definition of success.

One of the greatest discoveries in modern times to aid in understanding the Bible was treaties (covenants) between ancient Near Eastern kings and their subjects. When the structure of these ancient covenants was laid down on top of Deuteronomy, it was found that they matched exactly. Deuteronomy follows the form of a covenant between a king (God) and His subjects (Israel). The basic stipulations are found in the laws (summarized in the Ten Commandments; Deuteronomy 5:6-21). The King promised blessings for following His laws (Deuteronomy 28:1-14) and curses for disobeying them (Deuteronomy 28:15-68). Israel professed allegiance to the King and His covenant (Deuteronomy 29) and was granted life as a result (Deuteronomy 30:19-20).

COURAGE WHEN FAILURE DEFEATS YOU

Selected Scriptures

*In this lesson we learn what to do
when we don't understand what God says or does.*

OUTLINE

Nothing infuriates us like sitting on hold and listening to elevator music on the telephone, only to discover when we talk to a real person that they can't help us. Sometimes God doesn't speak when and how we want Him to. For those situations, we need courage to trust Him anyway.

I.   **Perplexing Problems**
    A. A Question That Must Be Answered
    B. An Answer That Must Be Questioned

II. **Powerful Principles**

III. **Persistent Praise**

IV. **Three Applications**
    A. When You Think God Doesn't Hear You, He Is Always Very Near You
    B. When You Don't Know What to Do, Remember Who You Know
    C. When You Can't See God in Your Problems, You Will Discover Him in Your Praise

Y ou are probably like me in at least one way: There have been times I've sought the Lord's help in some matter only to receive silence back as an answer. Meanwhile, the problem grew more intense.

Maybe you've prayed for a loved one to be saved or a wayward child to come to his senses. Maybe you've prayed for a job when you've needed one or for a friend to be healed of an illness. Sometimes we pray and pray, and it seems nothing happens. It seems we are all alone in the universe with our problem, and God is far, far away.

You may be relieved to know this is not a modern problem. A prophet named Habakkuk wrestled with why we sometimes call on God and He doesn't answer. In fact, Habakkuk is called the "Doubting Thomas" (John 20:24-25) of the Old Testament. Habakkuk's book is different from the other books of the Old Testament prophets. The other prophets delivered messages from God to His people, Israel. But Habakkuk's book is three chapters of dialogue between the prophet and his God. We get to listen in on a conversation in which Habakkuk unburdens his soul to God; a "Q&A" session in which Habakkuk wonders if God is being attentive to his requests.

Habakkuk means "to embrace" in Hebrew. That is a wonderful thought to hold onto as you read Habakkuk's story. Even though he didn't understand God's actions (or lack of them), he still embraced his God.

Perplexing Problems

Habakkuk's story begins in Habakkuk 1:1-11 with a question that needed to be answered and an answer that needed to be questioned.

A Question That Must Be Answered

Here is Habakkuk's basic question for God: "O Lord, how long shall I cry, and You will not hear?" (verse 2) But it was not just the fact that Habakkuk had asked God a question to which he had not received an answer. It was the content of the question that was vexing:

For plundering and violence are before me;
There is strife, and contention arises.
Therefore the law is powerless,
And justice never goes forth.
For the wicked surround the righteous;
Therefore perverse judgment proceeds (verses 3-4).

The prophet Habakkuk lived during a time when the people of God had moved far away from the godly principles upon which their nation had been founded. He cried out against the injustice and wickedness, and nobody seemed to be listening—not even God. Habakkuk was very frustrated: How could a holy God look upon such wickedness, and not do something about it? But this question is not just for Habakkuk's day, is it? We look at the wickedness in our culture and wonder why God does not provide some relief. We cry out with the same words as Habakkuk: "O Lord, how long shall I cry, and You will not hear?"

John Phillips, in his commentary on Habakkuk, compared our culture with Habakkuk's:

> Today the law is emasculated. Criminals are coddled; the death sentence has been abolished in many places and judges slap repeat offenders on the wrist. Pleas of temporary insanity can absolve perpetrators from penalties for the most heinous crimes. Hardened criminals can play the appeals system for years and escape with punishments far lighter than their deeds deserve. Court cases are deferred until the memories of witnesses become hazy. Judges are inconsistent, often open to bribes, and frequently more concerned with protecting than punishing the guilty.

> The absolute standards of morality mandated by God's law have given place to relative morality, which accommodates wickedness. The wholesale slaughter of unborn babies by abortion is condoned on the grounds of a woman's right to choose. Pornography flourishes under the guise of freedom of the press. Syndicated crime, drug trafficking, prostitution, child abuse, political corruption, and blind foreign policy contribute to the growing moral weakness of the nation.

> Such is the permissive society we see, and such was the permissive society Habakkuk saw. He came to the conclusion that the wicked outnumbered the righteous.[1]

Nothing stretches our faith any more than the apparent indifference of God! The silence of God has given many ungodly sinners an excuse to blaspheme and many weary believers the temptation to give up their faith. To Habakkuk, God was indifferent to his situation.

An Answer That Must Be Questioned

But God did eventually respond to Habakkuk, yet it was an answer with which Habakkuk was not satisfied. God's answer raised even more questions for Habakkuk!

You can read God's answer in verses 5-11, but let me summarize it this way: God said, "All right, Habakkuk, here's what I'll do. I'm going to raise up the Chaldeans and use them as my rod of judgment to discipline the people of Israel" (verse 6, paraphrased).

If you have ever prayed about something, then wished you hadn't prayed once the answer came . . . . then you can imagine Habakkuk's feeling—only quadrupled!

Here's the problem Habakkuk had with God's answer: The Chaldeans were the most wicked nation on earth. If anyone battling the Chaldeans looked like they would be captured, they would commit suicide rather than become Chaldean prisoners. The cruelty of the Chaldeans was known far and wide.

So, God's answer meant that He was going to use a nation much more wicked than Israel to judge Israel. That didn't make any sense at all to Habakkuk. But that is exactly what God did when He sent the Babylonians (Chaldeans) to destroy Jerusalem and carry the Jews into captivity to Babylon.

Throughout history we find examples of God using the more-wicked to judge the less-wicked. That is a mystery from our human perspective, but God keeps the scales balanced according to His own purposes. For the moment, Habakkuk was baffled by God's choices.

POWERFUL PRINCIPLES

It was going to take some explaining for Habakkuk to come to grips with God's reasoning on the subject of Israel's wickedness. So, from perplexing problems we go to powerful principles. Habakkuk responds to God again:

> You are of purer eyes than to behold evil,
> And cannot look on wickedness.
> Why do You look on those who deal treacherously,
> And hold Your tongue when the wicked devours
> A person more righteous than he? (verse 13)

Why would a holy God judge His own people by using a nation that was much more wicked than they were?

Habakkuk rehearsed in his prayer the character of God. He knew God was "from everlasting" (verse 12); He existed before this problem and will exist after it is solved. He knew God was holy and "cannot look on wickedness" (verse 13). He didn't understand a holy God using an unholy nation as a tool of judgment—but he knew that doesn't change God's holiness.

Here's the question for Habakkuk and for us: What do we do when we're caught in the swamp of imponderable things? You seek God, and His answer is delayed. When His answer comes, you don't understand it. We get in the elevator on the first floor and God is on the twenty-fifth floor. There's a great gap between where we are (our ways) and where He is (His ways).

Here's what I do in those situations: I concentrate on what I know, not on what I don't know. I concentrate on God's character, not on His choices. I concentrate on the good things I know He has done, not on the things I think He might do or hasn't done. I concentrate on His love, mercy, goodness, power—and most of all on the attribute I appreciate more than all others: His long-suffering patience.

There is a camp in California called Hume Lake where I went to preach in the summers. It is a beautiful setting in the mountains, filled with all kinds of scenery and adventures. As I hiked around the lake, I discovered swampy parts where the water turned the ground mushy. At first, it seemed like there was no way to cross these swampy parts. But then I would find a firm place to step, then from there another then another until, one step at a time, I had made my way to firmer ground on the other side of the bog. That's how I see these situations—we take them one step at a time, standing on what we know is firm, then moving to another firm truth, until we make it through.

In the midst of every imponderable situation there will be firm truths—powerful principles—upon which you can stand. Go from one to another as God brings them to mind, and you will stay on firm ground until you're out of the swamp. If you don't move forward until the swamp is drained, you'll be stuck for a long time.

PERSISTENT PRAISE

We don't have the space in this short lesson to work all the way through Habakkuk and God's dialogue, so we'll fast-forward to chapter 3 to see where Habakkuk ends up. He finds himself able to offer persistent praise to God in spite of what he didn't understand about His actions. This section of Habakkuk is one of my favorite parts of the Bible.

Habakkuk's praise becomes even more significant when we realize that he might be a victim of the coming Chaldean war machine. But he is okay with that, as evidenced by his final words:

Though the fig tree may not blossom,
Nor fruit be on the vines;
Though the labor of the olive may fail,
And the fields yield no food;
Though the flock may be cut off from the fold,
And there be no herd in the stalls—
Yet I will rejoice in the Lord,
I will joy in the God of my salvation.
The Lord God is my strength;
He will make my feet like deer's feet,
And He will make me walk on my high hills (verses 17-19).

It is important to notice Habakkuk's use of the word "Selah" (3:3, 9, 13). These are the only uses of the word in the Old Testament outside of its 71 uses in Psalms. No one is exactly sure what the word means, though it seems to be a musical notation of some sort, indicating the words were to be set to music. "Selah" occurs at the end of verse 13 and, at the end of the book, following verse 19, we have these words: "To the Chief Musician. With my stringed instruments." I believe this last paragraph of Habakkuk was a hymn, a song of praise.

In spite of the fact that the fig tree may not blossom, there may not be any fruit on the vine, the fields are barren, and the flocks are diminished, Habakkuk says, "I will joy in the God of my salvation." William Barclay, in his commentary on Habakkuk, says that "this expression in the Hebrew literally says, 'I will spin around in the joy of my God.'" Those are no longer the words of a despondent and confused prophet, but the words of one who is trusting in his God in spite of what he doesn't understand.

John Phillips, whom I quoted earlier, says about Habakkuk's song: "One of the best ways to instill a truth into the heart, soul, and conscience of an individual or nation is to set that truth to music, to incorporate it into a great hymn. So Habakkuk sets his poem to music, dedicated it 'to the chief singer,' and picked up one of his own 'stringed instruments.'"[2]

Habakkuk is following a thread here that runs throughout the Old Testament. The three Hebrew young men told Nebuchadnezzar that, even if God didn't rescue them from the fiery furnace, they wouldn't worship the king's idols. We have Job saying, "Even if God slays me, yet will I trust Him." And here we have Habakkuk rising above his circumstances and his understanding, saying, "If the world comes unglued . . . if I lose everything I have . . . if our economy is destroyed . . . I am still going to joy in the God of my salvation."

THREE APPLICATIONS

From Habakkuk's experience, here are three perspectives that you can take to the spiritual bank—three truths that will stand you in good stead when you have questions for God that need answering, and you feel like questioning God's answers.

When You Think God Doesn't Hear You, He Is Always Very Near You

The first application is this: When you think God doesn't hear you, it is not because He is far away. God is always nearer to you than you can imagine. Just because He doesn't give you an immediate reply to your question doesn't mean He is far away.

Habakkuk allowed his circumstances to color his view of God's presence. He thought God had forgotten all about him and his problems. He was crying out to God because of the indifference of the people. Heaven seemed silent; but all along, God had His plan in place. He did not begin to respond to the sin of Israel when Habakkuk started to cry out to Him. God already knew what He was going to do. Even when His prophet felt forgotten, God was in control.

You may not think God cares about your problem, but He does. Even now, because you are His child, He is working in your behalf. Your prayers will take you into His plan and help you to understand what He is doing in due time. Never stop praying on the basis of your feelings. Your feelings will betray you every time. When you think God doesn't hear, He is always very near.

When You Don't Know What to Do, Remember Who You Know

There is something vastly more important in life than knowing what to do—it's remembering who you know. The well-worn phrase that we hear used in politics—"It's not what you know, it's who you know"—has application here.

Habakkuk's final worship song to God is the key to the book. He knew who God was, and that provided the basis for him to work his way through the circumstances he did not understand. Habakkuk teaches us this important lesson: You worship the one you trust, and you trust the one you know! Habakkuk knew his God and, because of that, he could trust Him when he did not understand what He was doing.

Hudson Taylor, founder of the China Inland Mission, probably made the greatest impact on world missions of anyone in the modern era. He is considered to be the father of modern faith missions. I commend to you the two books on Hudson Taylor written by his daughter-in-law: *The Growth of a Soul* and *The Growth of a Work of God*. A third, Hudson Taylor's *Spiritual Secret*, provides a helpful distillation of Taylor's life and ministry. Every Christian today should be familiar with the life of this great missionary who had such a burden for the Chinese people.

In his later years, when Hudson Taylor was old and frail, his son and daughter-in-law traveled extensively with him in China. They would travel for hours in a cart over rough cobblestone roads and arrive late at night seeking room for the night in a Chinese inn. The inns had large rooms where travelers slept on mats, all in the same room. They would try to find a corner for their father to sleep in where he would not be disturbed.

But invariably, the next morning, they would find that Hudson Taylor had woken before dawn, lit a candle, and was worshiping God. His goal in life was always to be up worshiping God when the sun came up. Hudson Taylor testified in his writings that the one thing that sustained him as he faced the challenges and pressures of his ministry—"the one thing that gave me an even gait through it all," he said—was the fact that every morning before the sun came up, he rose to worship God. In worshiping God, he found the strength, the power, and the energy that left a mark upon his world.

Hudson Taylor knew that when you don't know what to do, you remember who you know in order to make it through this world. None of us knows what that means. As a nation of individuals, we are faced today with the threat of terrorist attacks of unknown proportions and effects. But we can live with that uncertainty—and even the reality—if we know God.

Habakkuk did not know what would happen when the Chaldeans came over the horizon toward Jerusalem. But he knew God did. Therefore, it was better to know God than to know what the Chaldeans might do. After all, what could he do to prevent their coming? Far better to know the One who could prevent the destruction from happening. If God allowed it, there must be a good reason. Better to know God than to know the future.

When You Can't See God in Your Problems, You Will Discover Him in Your Praise

Finally, there is a power and permanent perspective that will allow you to see God at all times, providing you are willing to praise Him: When you can't see Him in your problems, you will discover Him in your praise.

In the *Pentecostal Evangel* magazine, J. K. Gressett wrote about a man named Samuel who settled on a farm in the Arizona desert with his wife and children.

> One night a fierce storm struck with rain, hail, and high wind. [With our annual mudslides, floods, and wildfires, those of us who live in California can identify.] At daybreak, feeling sick and fearing what he might find, Samuel went out to survey the loss.

> The hail had beaten the garden and truck patch into the ground; the house was partially unroofed, the henhouse had blown away, and dead chickens were scattered about. Destruction and devastation were everywhere.

> While standing dazed, evaluating the mess and wondering about the future, he heard a stirring in the lumber pile that was the remains of the henhouse. A rooster was climbing up through the debris, and he didn't stop climbing until he had mounted the highest board in the pile. That old rooster was dripping wet, and most of his feathers were blown away. But as the sun came over the eastern horizon, he flapped his bony wings and proudly crowed. That wet old, bare rooster could still crow when he saw the morning sun. And like that rooster, our world may be falling apart, we may have lost everything; but if we trust in God, we'll be able to see the light of God's goodness, pick ourselves out of the rubble, and sing the Lord's praise.[3]

We will not only sing His praise; we will, like the rooster, sing it from the highest place!

So remember Habakkuk the next time you are faced with a perplexing problem and God has not answered you in a way you understand—or hasn't answered you at all. Find the firm truths, the powerful principles, about God that you know; and stand on those. Go from one to another, praising Him with every step. And keep in mind the permanent perspectives about Him that never change. You, too, will find yourself crowing about Him from the heights!

Notes

1. John Phillips, *Exploring the Minor Prophets* (Grand Rapids: Kregel Publications, 1998), 206-207.

2. Ibid.

3. J. K. Gressett, "Take Courage," *Pentecostal Evangel* (April 30, 1989), 6.

1. Read Habakkuk 1:1-13.

   a. What was Habakkuk's question for God? (verse 2)

   b. What did Habakkuk see happening around him at that time? (verses 3-4)

   c. Does what was happening around Habakkuk seem similar or different to what is happening in our world today? Explain your answer.

   d. What was God's answer to Habakkuk? (verses 5-6)

   e. How did God describe the Chaldeans in verses 6-11?

f. Why did this answer raise even more questions in Habakkuk's mind?

g. How did Habakkuk describe God in verses 12-13?

h. Why is it important to focus and meditate on God's character when you don't understand what He is doing in your life?

2. Read Habakkuk 3:17-19.

a. Why do you think Habakkuk was able to offer persistent praise to God in spite of not understanding His ways?

b. How has praising God helped you to persevere during difficult times in your life?

c. Habakkuk chose to rejoice in God, even if what difficulties occurred? (verse 17)

d. In the greater context of Habakkuk's situation, what makes his praise even more significant?

e. Habakkuk had confidence that God would do what for him? (verses 18-19)

f. In what ways did Habakkuk's attitude change from the beginning of chapter 1 to the end of chapter 3?

GROUP QUESTIONS

1. Read Habakkuk 1:1-13 as a group.

   a. Discuss the questions Habakkuk asked God in verses 2-3. Have you ever asked God a similar question? If so, share your situation with the group.

   b. Was God's answer in verses 5-6 what Habakkuk expected? Why or why not?

   c. The Chaldeans are described in verses 6-11. What adjectives are used to describe them? To what are they compared?

   d. According to verse 9, what were the goals of the Chaldeans?

   e. How did Habakkuk describe God in verses 12-13?

2. Read Habakkuk 3:17-19 together.

   a. Why was Habakkuk able to offer persistent praise to God in spite of not understanding God's answer to him?

   b. Discuss the importance of Habakkuk's use of the word "Selah" earlier in chapter 3. (See verses 3, 9, 13.) How does the use of "Selah" give us a greater understanding of this passage?

   c. Habakkuk chose to rejoice in the Lord, even if what happened? (verse 17)

3. What caused Habakkuk to think God had forgotten about him and his problems?

4. Why is it important to study God's character and how does that knowledge help us during difficult times?

5. Describe a time in your life when you chose to praise God in the midst of a trial. Share your answer with the group.

DID YOU KNOW?

Habakkuk is the grandfather of the Protestant Reformation, begun in 1517. Though Habakkuk and the Reformation were separated by about two thousand years, they are vitally connected by the Word of God. In Habakkuk 2:4, the prophet wrote in his hour of confusion that "the just shall live by his faith." Though he didn't understand what God was doing, he would trust God by faith. Two millennia later, when a German monk named Martin Luther was desperately trying to find God by doing good works, he read Romans 1:17 where Paul quotes Habakkuk 2:4: "As it is written, 'The just shall live by faith.'" That truth was the spark that set Martin Luther free from sin and dead works and sparked the Protestant Reformation.

COURAGE WHEN FRIENDS DISAPPOINT YOU

2 Timothy 4:9-18

In this lesson we learn how to avoid discouragement when friends disappoint us.

OUTLINE

There is a risk that comes with close friendships: the potential for disappointment. Is the solution not to have friends? No, the solution is to learn how to maintain courage even if we are deserted. We can learn from the last days of the apostle Paul's life how to be strong even when alone.

I. **Facing the Challenges of Disappointment**
   A. Difficulty
   B. Despair
   C. Defection

II. **Finding Courage for Disappointment**
   A. Physical Encouragement
   B. Personal Encouragement
   C. Mental Encouragement
   D. Spiritual Encouragement

Pepper Rogers was the football coach for UCLA many years ago. He told the story of a particularly bad season his team was having. It was so bad, he said, that it began to upset his home life. Even his wife thought he was doing a terrible job. He said, "My dog was my only friend, and I told my wife that a man needs at least two friends. So she went out and bought me another dog."

Look up in a book of quotations and you'll find various definitions of "friend"—and they all probably have a measure of truth to them. But we need to learn about friendship from God's perspective, not the world's. In this lesson, we will study the difficult question of how to respond when friends disappoint us.

A book I read on friendship pointed out four levels of friends in life.

First, there are contact friends. These are people you run into along the way in life. You may see them on a fairly regular basis—like the checkout clerk at your grocery store—but you really don't know them. You may not even know the names of these contact friends.

Then there are casual friends. These may be people with whom you have a slightly deeper relationship—people at work, people in the neighborhood. You spend enough time around them to know their names and talk about surface issues, but that's as deep as it goes.

At a deeper level are close friends. These are people with whom you share common goals in life. Perhaps a business coworker with whom you've become close, a friend you've gotten to know through a church ministry, or a member of a Bible study or other social network.

Finally, there are committed friends. People usually only have a couple of these—people who care enough about you to confront you or correct you, a person who will stick by your side through thick and thin, sick and sin. You are truly blessed if you have even one of these kinds of friends.

I am always amazed when I read the New Testament at how many friends the apostle Paul had. We tend to think of Paul as a task-person, not a people-person, not someone who had time to make and keep close friendships. He was a missionary who traveled extensively, he was an author who committed time to writing detailed letters to new churches, he was an itinerant preacher, a theologian, counselor, church planter . . . when did Paul have time to cultivate friendships?

The best evidence of Paul's ability to be a good friend is found in the last chapter of Romans. As he closes the epistle, he mentions 34 people by name by way of commendation or extending greetings to them in Rome. And the amazing thing is that when he wrote the letter to Rome, he had never even been there! Yet he knew many people in that church.

Another good example of Paul's friendship skills is found in the passage we will study in this lesson: 2 Timothy 4. In verses 9-21, Paul mentions the names of 17 people. In addition, he mentions two others in chapter 1. Letters are a good place to discover the soul of a person since, as the ancient writer Demetrius said, "Everyone reveals his soul in his letters."[1] And that's what we learn about Paul. In this second letter to his young protégé, Timothy, Paul reveals his heart.

FACING THE CHALLENGES OF DISAPPOINTMENT

This was a challenging time for Paul. Second Timothy was written near the end of his life, and we're looking at the last chapter of this, his last letter. He mentions people in his letter to Timothy who are no longer standing with him in the Gospel. What causes people to abandon us as their friends?

Difficulty

Paul was in prison when he wrote this letter—a good place to look up and find your friends have deserted you. Nobody wants to admit they're the friend of a person who is in jail or prison. Why was he imprisoned?

Nero, the Roman emperor at the time, was actively persecuting Christians. He had set Rome on fire in A.D. 64 and then put the blame on Christians as a reason to persecute them. Life was awful under Nero. Even many Roman citizens were committing suicide rather than live under the moral decay so rampant in Nero's Rome. Paul would get word in his Roman prison cell of Christians who perished under Nero. Some were killed in the Colosseum. Some were set on fire to serve as human torches in Nero's garden. Nero was a depraved ruler, and Paul could do nothing but pray for his friends who were suffering while he contemplated his own fate.

Difficult times in our lives often separate us from our friends. Think of those in the military stationed abroad . . . think of those who are going through a divorce . . . think of those with a terminal or debilitating illness . . . think of moving to a new community and being on the outside. In all these situations, people are often afraid to draw near to us. They don't know what to say; and rather than say the wrong thing, they stay away. It's understandable, but it doesn't make it any easier. We wish we had friends who would break through the barrier of discomfort and stay close to us regardless of the situation.

It's hard to imagine the apostle Paul, the most important person in the Christian Church, sitting alone in a prison cell. But even Paul was separated from many of his friends. When we go through difficult times, we don't have to wonder who our friends are. We will find out pretty quickly by who shows up to ask about us and our needs.

Despair

Scholars believe that Paul's final imprisonment in Rome was in the dreaded Mamertine Prison. (This is not the same imprisonment we read about at the end of the book of Acts. He was released from that first imprisonment and later rearrested and imprisoned in the Mamertine Prison until he ultimately suffered death under Nero.) I visited the remains of this prison on a trip to Rome once, and it does not give the impression of being a pleasant place. Prisoners' lives held little value in Rome.

Paul knew he was about to die. He had lived through his first hearing before the emperor and escaped both this figurative "lion" and the lions in the Colosseum because he was a Roman citizen (2 Timothy 4:17; see Acts 21:39; 22:28). But public and official sentiment against Christians was high, and Paul knew his days were short: "For I am already being poured out as a drink offering, and the time of my departure is at hand" (2 Timothy 4:6).

Paul did not sink completely into despair. He felt he had kept the commission given him by Christ to take the Gospel to the Gentiles: "I have fought the good fight, I have finished the race, I have kept the faith. Finally, there is laid up for me the crown of righteousness, which the Lord, the righteous Judge, will give to me on that Day, and not to me only but also to all who have loved His appearing" (2 Timothy 4:7-8).

Tradition tells us that Paul was beheaded on the Ostian Way about three miles outside the (then) city of Rome. The Christian historian Eusebius tells us that Paul and the apostle Peter were executed on the same day. Though we can't document the details of Paul's death, we do know that Second Timothy was his last letter. He was isolated, alone, staring death in the face. Sometimes situations of despair cause us to be friendless.

Defection

Sometimes it's not our problems that keep people away—it's theirs! Paul's greatest pain was not being in a prison cell; it was that his friends in Asia had turned against him. Paul says in 2 Timothy 1:15 that Phygellus and Hermogenes, along with the rest of his friends in Asia, had turned against him.

Reading through the last verses of 2 Timothy 4 is like reading a litany of defection and desertion: Demas had forsaken Paul . . . Crescens had gone to Galatia and Titus to Dalmatia. Tychicus, Paul had sent to Ephesus. "Alexander the coppersmith did [Paul] much harm" (verse 14). Erastus stayed in Corinth and Trophimus was sick in Miletus.

At his first arraignment before the emperor, "No one stood with [him], but all forsook [him]" (verse 16). You can almost feel the pain of loneliness in Paul's words. But there was a bright ray of friendship amidst the darkness of those who had defected: "Only Luke is with me" (verse 11). Luke, the author of one of the Gospels and the book of Acts, was Paul's physician and traveling companion on his missionary journeys. He was a faithful friend who remained by Paul's side in Rome, apparently until the end.

A noted commentator, Bishop Handley Moule, wrote about Paul at this time in his life: "For the great apostle Paul was also a creature of flesh and blood, a man of like nature and passions with ourselves. Although he has finished his course and is awaiting his crown, he is still a frail human being with ordinary human needs."[2]

That's why I love Second Timothy. It is a glimpse into the real world of the apostle Paul who was a person like you and me with hurts and longings and desires. And yes, he even got lonely for friendship at the end of his life.

Let me give you a bit more background on two of the people Paul mentions in chapter 4: Demas and Alexander.

Demas is mentioned three times in the New Testament. Once he is mentioned along with Luke in a kind of "neutral" context (Colossians 4:14). A second time he is mentioned as one of Paul's fellow laborers (Philemon 24). And the third time he is mentioned, here in 2 Timothy 4, we are told that he had abandoned Paul. Paul writes that Demas "loved this present world" and departed for Thessalonica (verse 10).

How devastating this must have been for Paul, the man who had probably discipled Demas and brought him along in the faith. Some believe that with Paul in jail, the price just got too high for Demas; and he escaped to protect himself. We don't know. "Defected" is the word Paul used—and it's a strong one.

Alexander was the second man Paul mentioned with extra effort: "[Alexander] did me much harm" (verse 14). Literally, that sentence reads, "He informed many evil things against me." Some have suggested that Alexander acted like a Judas, informing on Paul to the authorities who arrested him a second time and put him in prison. That theory at least goes along with Paul's warning to Timothy: "You also must beware of him, for he has greatly resisted our words" (2 Timothy 4:15). Paul is saying, "Watch out for Alexander—he's nothing but trouble!"

Disappointment with others is part of leadership and part of life. The higher your commitment to Christ, the farther away from "the crowd" you remove yourself. There will be those whose commitment is not as high and who will ultimately desert you or disappoint you. Sometimes they will be people into whom you poured your life, and you will be devastated. But it is part of the calling to discipleship. You cannot worry about what others do; you can only stay focused on not deserting the Lord and others yourself.

What did the apostle John write about the Lord Jesus Himself? "He came to His own, and His own did not receive Him" (John 1:11). So if you are disappointed by those close to you, at least you are in good company.

Here's an interesting thought from the great preacher and missions leader, A. B. Simpson: "Often the crowd does not recognize a leader until he is gone, and then they build a monument for him with the same stones they threw at him during his life."

FINDING COURAGE FOR DISAPPOINTMENT

While there are some discouraging things to read in this last chapter of Second Timothy, there are some really encouraging words as well. In fact, it is from this same chapter that we find the courage to rebound from disappointments with friends.

Physical Encouragement

Paul was stuck deep in the dark and damp Mamertine Prison, and winter was coming on. He included a request in this letter to Timothy for the "cloak that I left with Carpus at Troas" (verse 13). And then, as a footnote, he wrote, "Do your utmost to come before winter" (verse 21).

Paul's cloak was probably akin to our poncho—a large, heavy, wool blanket type affair with a hole in the middle for your head. In a day when all of us probably have more coats than we need, it is amazing to think of Paul having only one, and it being hundreds of miles away in Asia Minor!

I think this got included in the Bible to remind us that there are needs we have that can impact our lives, physically and spiritually. Sometimes it takes more than prayer to encourage a brother or sister. We need to minister to their physical needs as well. You and I both know that Paul would be more encouraged if he could stay warm than if he were freezing cold during the winter.

The area surrounding our church was devastated by wildfires in 2003; many people lost their homes and everything they owned. If our church had gone up into the mountains and set up a big tent and passed out Bibles and tracts and offered to tell people about Jesus . . . I shudder to think of what a terrible testimony that would have been. People needed to be ministered to physically—food, clothing, shelter, money. And that's what we tried to provide for those who needed it. Of course, if a spiritual need arose, we tried to meet that need as well. But we wanted people to know that God cares about their humanity—what they needed to stay alive and be encouraged enough to start over and rebuild.

Paul was cold and wanted his coat! There's nothing unspiritual about that. Let's look to the physical needs people have as a way to rebuild their courage.

Personal Encouragement

Not only was Paul cold, he was lonely. He needed to see a friendly face. He asked Timothy to come to him quickly (verse 9). And then he asked Timothy to grab John Mark and bring him along too (verse 11). Remember Mark? He was the one who greatly disappointed Paul earlier in his ministry by deserting Paul and Barnabas on the first missionary journey (Acts 13:13). But now Paul wants to have Mark with him, "for he is useful to me for ministry" (verse 11). Finally, he tells Timothy to come before the weather turns bad in winter, making travel all the more difficult (verse 21).

What do all these snippets of insight into Paul's life tell us? That in our times of disappointment, we need friends and companions to come alongside us. Christ is always with us, true. And that satisfies our need to know that God is guiding and encouraging us. But human relationships are critical as well. God demonstrated that by sending His Son to earth as a man—to be a friend to His disciples (John 15:15).

Timothy was Paul's child in the faith. Paul had mentored Timothy for years and brought him along to the point that Timothy was ready to lead the church in Ephesus. Paul had probably grown closer to Timothy in a way he had not with any of his other colaborers. Luke was a peer, an older friend. But Timothy brought the energy and encouragement of youth, and Paul wanted to see him.

Note: What we're talking about here is a companion, not a counselor. When someone is discouraged, you don't have to preach him a sermon. Just be a friend and encourage him by saying, "I care for you, and I'm here for however I can help."

Mental Encouragement

Paul needed warmth and he needed companionship. But he also needed mental stimulation and encouragement. Note that he asks Timothy to bring to him "the books, especially the parchments" (verse 13).

The difference between the two was that the "books" were likely made from papyrus, the reed that was pounded together into flat sheets, then dried, while the "parchments" were likely animal skins that were cleaned, stretched, and dried. Both were common writing surfaces used in Paul's day. The "books" could have been Paul's personal papers, his correspondence, and writing materials, while the "parchments" were probably copies of Old Testament Scriptures, perhaps the Greek version or other sacred texts like the collected teachings of Christ.

The point of this request was that Paul wanted to use his hours in prison redemptively. He wasn't depressed, staring at the wall. He wanted to redeem the time and use it to further his knowledge of the Scriptures or his own ministry of writing. All of us find ourselves with odd minutes or hours to fill on occasion. Or perhaps we have protracted periods during an illness or unemployment. Sometimes study and mental work can be a relief or diversion during periods of isolation.

But more than a diversion, the Word of God in all its forms— written, video, audio, music, books—can keep our spiritual eyes focused on God at a time when we might be tempted to lose courage. Even if we don't feel like it, we should do it as a matter of discipline. More likely than not, your feelings will catch up with your actions; your will leads the way, and your emotions follow. That happens to me every time I read the Word as a matter of choice instead of a matter of feeling.

The reason we need to stay in the Word continually is that there will never be a time in our lives when problems aren't present. With people come problems. So if you have been deserted by those you thought were with you, keep your mind engaged by staying in the Word.

Spiritual Encouragement

Finally, Paul needed spiritual encouragement, and he got that from the Lord: "But the Lord stood with me and strengthened me.... And the Lord will deliver me from every evil work and preserve me for His heavenly kingdom. To Him be glory forever and ever. Amen!" (verses 17-18)

Those are not the words of a depressed or discouraged—albeit deserted—man. Paul was alone physically, but the Lord was with him. When he stood before the emperor, the Lord stood with him and delivered him "out of the mouth of the lion" (verse 17). And he anticipated the Lord delivering him to heaven when his life on earth ended.

If you are disappointed in friends . . . if some have deserted you . . . if you are isolated and alone for any reason . . . God is with you. Take courage from the fact that He is the Friend who never leaves you nor forsakes you.

Notes

1. Demetrius quoted by William Ramsey, *The Letters to Timothy, Titus, and Philemon*, Revised edition (Philadelphia: Westminster Press, 1975), XIII.

2. Handley C. G. Moule, *The Second Epistle to Timothy*, the Devotional Commentary Series (London: Religious Tract Society, 1905), 15.

1. Has a friend ever disappointed you or abandoned you? If so, describe what happened.

2. Read 2 Timothy 4:6-22.

   a. Where was Paul when he wrote Second Timothy?

   b. Who was the ruler of the Roman empire at this time and how did he treat Christians?

   c. What insight do verses 6-8 give you as to what Paul understood about his future?

   d. Make a list of the people Paul mentioned in this passage. What does this list teach you about Paul's view of friendship?

e. Who was the person who was still with Paul in Rome? (verse 11)

f. Where had some of Paul's other friends gone? (verses 10, 12)

g. Why did Timothy need to beware of Alexander the coppersmith? (verses 14-15)

h. What two requests did Paul have for Timothy in verse 13?

i. Why were these items important to Paul?

j. How can physical items provide you with encouragement when you are discouraged? Can you think of a physical item that encourages you on difficult days? If so, what is the item?

k. What does Paul's requests for "the books, especially the parchments" (verse 13) tell you about how he was using his time in prison?

l. How was Paul encouraged spiritually in his time of need? (verses 17-18)

m. What final instruction did Paul give Timothy in verse 21? How is this connected to his request for his cloak in verse 13?

3. What is one way you can encourage a friend this week?

GROUP QUESTIONS

1. If comfortable, share with the group about a time when a friend disappointed or abandoned you.

2. Read 2 Timothy 4:6-22 as a group.

   a. Discuss what Paul was experiencing and preparing for when he wrote Second Timothy. What types of persecution were Christians facing during that time? What did Paul understand about his own fate?

   b. How many people does Paul name in this passage?

   c. What does this teach us about how much Paul valued friendship?

   d. Who was Demas and how was he described in Paul's letter to Philemon? (See Colossians 4:14 and Philemon 24.)

e. Why did Demas abandon Paul and where did he go? (verse 10)

f. Why must this have been devastating for Paul?

g. Paul requested that Timothy bring his cloak and "the books, especially the parchments" (verse 13) with him. Why were those items necessary and important to Paul?

h. Why is it important to encourage people by meeting their physical needs? List some ways you, as a group, can encourage others this week by meeting their physical needs.

i. Who was with Paul during his first defense? (verses 16-17)

j. What was Paul confident of in verse 18?

3. Review the "Did You Know?" section of the lesson.

   a. Which of the friendships mentioned in this section stands out to you and why?

   b. How does viewing friendship as a covenant term challenge you in your own friendships?

DID YOU KNOW?

Friendship, as used often in the Bible, is a covenant term. Abraham, with whom God entered into a covenant, was called the friend of God (2 Chronicles 20:7; Isaiah 41:8; James 2:23). David and Jonathan, the son of Saul, were best friends and entered into a covenant of mutual provision and protection (1 Samuel 18:1-4). They epitomized the "friend who sticks closer than a brother" (Proverbs 18:24). And when Jesus Christ prepared to leave this earth, He changed the term by which He addressed His disciples: "No longer do I call you servants . . . but I have called you friends, for all things that I heard from My Father I have made known to you" (John 15:15).

COURAGE WHEN FATIGUE DRAINS YOU

Isaiah 40:28-31

In this lesson we discover how to gain new strength by waiting on God.

OUTLINE

We live in a world where frantic rushing is the norm. Every silent space is filled with noise of some kind: traffic, television, radio, music, conversation. We are fearful of the silent, empty spaces and places. And yet that is where we must wait in order to meet God and gain strength.

I. **The Symbol of Courageous Strength Is Soaring**

II. **The Secret of Courageous Strength Is Waiting**
   A. Waiting Results in Perception
   B. Waiting Results in Protection
   C. Waiting Results in Perspective
   D. Waiting Results in Provision
   E. Waiting Results in Power

III. **The Source of Courageous Strength Is God**

America is enraged—but for all the wrong reasons. Instead of being enraged over the decline of morality in our country, we're enraged over sporting events, drivers, and airline flight attendants who don't cater to our every need. Hardly a week goes by that the news doesn't report some incident of "rage." There was a huge brawl between players and fans at a professional basketball game, and the very next day a similar brawl at a college football game.

A San Diego newspaper carried this report in November 2004:

> The Surgeon General's Office doesn't put warning labels on people's driver's licenses, but maybe it should. A nation-wide survey by Farmers Insurance Group found that fourteen percent of drivers said they had shouted at or engaged in a horn-honking match with another motorist, ten percent admitted to intentionally cutting off others in traffic, and four percent confessed to keeping a weapon in the car for protection against others on the road. "We actually had twenty-four people tell us they'd gotten into fistfights," Farmers spokeswoman Mary Flynn said of the survey of 1001 drivers.[1]

Author C. Leslie Charles made this observation about how people function in America today: "Cell phones, pagers, and high tech devices allow us to be interrupted anywhere, at any time. This constant accessibility and compulsive use of technology fragments what little time we do have, adding to our sense of urgency, emergency, and overload. There is never a time for us to be alone."[2]

This is a perfect introduction into our final lesson in this series on courage. When life is so hectic and fragmented, how do we find time to resupply our reservoirs of courage and peace so that we don't become part of the "culture of rage" that is all around us?

THE SYMBOL OF COURAGEOUS STRENGTH IS SOARING

In this well-known passage, Isaiah 40:28-31, we discover a discipline that can transform the way we do life! Look at the passage from the bottom up—beginning with the last verse.

The symbol of courageous strength is the eagle: mounting up with wings like eagles, running and not being weary, walking and not fainting.

I once read an article that described three different ways birds fly.

First, some birds fly by simply flapping their wings to counteract the force of gravity. Hummingbirds are in this category, flapping their wings up to seventy times per second. This is commendable, but it seems to take so much effort and work! I'm supposed to be soaring like an eagle; but, a lot of the time, I'm flapping like crazy, wearing myself out.

Second, some birds fly by gliding. They flap until they get high enough, and they glide slowly back down to earth. This is more graceful than flapping, but it is temporary at best since, without more flapping, you hit the ground.

The third way is what we would call soaring. Only a few birds, like the eagle, have wings capable of capturing the lift of rising columns of heated air and riding them far into the sky without moving a muscle. Soaring is what Isaiah had in mind when he wrote the passage in chapter 40. Those who wait on the Lord will soar—"They shall mount up with wings like eagles" (verse 31).

I don't recommend flapping. Gliding is only a little better. Soaring is the picture of what it means to rest in God and let the wind of His Spirit lift us above the fray of the battles on this earth. Only by soaring will we be just as rested when we finish as when we began.

Some people think Isaiah is giving us a picture of the stages of life:

- Youth: soar like eagles
- Middle-age: run without getting weary
- Old age: walk without fainting

Others think he's telling us how to face different challenges in life:

- Crisis: we soar
- Normal ups and downs: run without getting weary
- Plodding day after day: walk without fainting

So, in every season of life and kind of situation, God gives us strength to live above the rage around us—never growing weary, never giving in.

THE SECRET OF COURAGEOUS STRENGTH IS WAITING

The question now is, How do we soar? We agree that soaring on the wind of the Spirit is the most efficient way for us to live the spiritual life—but how?

The secret is given by Isaiah: It is those who "wait on the Lord" (verse 31) who will soar. To wait means to pause, to soberly consider our own inadequacies and the Lord's all-sufficiency, to seek counsel and help from the Lord, and to hope in Him. Waiting involves submission to the Word of God and the will of God and the ways of God. Waiting is saying, "I'm not going to do this on my own. I'm going to do this in the strength that God provides. Lord, I'm going to let You be the updraft under my wings that causes me to be who You want me to be."

When I first moved to California from the Midwest, I didn't know anything about waiting. There was never a line at the bank or the grocery store or the gas station where I came from, and not much traffic to speak of. But when I got to California, I waited for everything that I didn't wait for in Indiana. I especially learned about waiting in restaurants. You wait to get in, wait to be seated, wait for the menu, wait to give your order, wait for your food, wait for dessert, wait for the check, and wait to pay your bill. I learned a new definition of who the "waiter" is in California restaurants!

Waiting is not easy for any of us, especially in our modern culture. However, Scripture gives us at least five benefits of waiting on the Lord.

Waiting Results in Perception

Psalm 25:4-5 says,

Show me Your ways, O Lord;
Teach me Your paths.
Lead me in Your truth and teach me,
For You are the God of my salvation;
On You I wait all the day.

"On You I wait" . . . . What is the psalmist waiting on? To be shown God's ways, paths, and truth. If you want to deepen your perception of spiritual truth, you will have to learn to wait.

Waiting Results in Protection

Psalm 33:20-21 says,

Our soul waits for the Lord;
He is our help and our shield.
For our heart shall rejoice in Him,
Because we have trusted in His holy name.

Protection is the result of waiting on the Lord. In fact, He is referred to in this passage as our shield, the one who protects us from everything that could come into our life and rob us of our peace and strength.

Waiting Results in Perspective

Psalm 37:7 says,

Rest in the Lord, and wait patiently for Him;
Do not fret because of him who prospers in his way,
Because of the man who brings wicked schemes to pass.

It's tempting to get upset over people who prosper and profit by doing bad things in this life. But this passage says the secret to getting over that is to wait on the Lord. In this case, wait for Him to balance the scales of justice which He will do one day. Waiting gives you an eternal perspective on temporal things.

Waiting Results in Provision

Lamentations 3:25-26 says,

The Lord is good to those who wait for Him,
To the soul who seeks Him.
It is good that one should hope and wait quietly
For the salvation of the Lord.

Who wouldn't want to experience more of God's goodness? Well, waiting on the Lord is the way to do it. The Lord is good to those who wait for Him.

Waiting Results in Power

Finally, Isaiah 40:31 says,

> But those who wait on the Lord
> Shall renew their strength;
> They shall mount up with wings like eagles.

We've already seen that waiting on the Lord provides the ability to soar in God's strength instead of flapping around in our own strength.

Those are the benefits of waiting on the Lord, but we still need to talk more about how we do it.

Daniel Goleman has written two widely-read books on the subject of emotional intelligence—how emotional intelligence is more important than mental, or cognitive, intelligence. He writes that at the heart of emotional intelligence is the ability to delay gratification and not live at the mercy of our impulses. He described a clinical test called the Marshmallow Test in which four-year-olds were the subjects. There is a marshmallow on the table, and the researcher tells the four-year-old he has to leave for a moment. The child is told he can either eat the one marshmallow now or wait until the researcher returns, at which time he can have two marshmallows. So there's the test: one marshmallow now or two in a few minutes?

A Stanford University research team tracked these children into adulthood. The ones who were able to delay their gratification grew up to be more socially competent, better able to cope with stress, and less likely to give up under pressure than those who couldn't delay their gratification. Those who couldn't wait, who ate the single marshmallow, grew up to be stubborn, indecisive, easily upset and frustrated, and resentful toward life.[3]

Given the impulsiveness of our culture and our insistence on having everything now, we would appear to be an emotionally immature people. We need to learn to slow down, to wait upon God's timing. When we feel a sense of panic or urgency arising in us, we need to know how to stop and wait. God is never in a panic or hurry; and if we are, then we're running off on our own without Him.

Sue Monk Kidd tells the story of taking a personal spiritual retreat at a monastery. She went out by a lake and tried to sit and be still and listen. She only lasted a few minutes before the need to act—do something!—drove her to get up and walk away. On her way back to her room, she saw a monk sitting perfectly still beneath a tree—a position he maintained for an hour. She found him later and asked how he could sit so still for so long. "I can't get used to the idea of doing nothing," she said.

The monk laughed and said, "That's because you've bought into the cultural myth that when you're waiting, you're doing nothing." Then he said, "When you're waiting, you're actually doing the most important something there is. You're allowing your soul to grow up. If you can't be still and wait, you can't become what God created you to be."[4]

Those words reflect the formulas found in Isaiah 30:15 and Psalm 46:10: Wait in quietness before the Lord and you will gain strength.

Silence is hard to find in our noisy world. Wayne Oats tells how to find it:

> Silence is not native to my world. Silence, more than likely, is a stranger to you and to your world, too. If you and I ever have silence in our noisy hearts, we're going to have to grow it. You can nurture silence in your noisy heart if you value it, cherish it, and are eager to nourish it.

THE SOURCE OF COURAGEOUS STRENGTH IS GOD

The symbol of courageous strength is the soaring eagle, and the secret of that strength is waiting on the Lord. It is now time to consider the source: God Himself. We arrive at the beginning of our passage in Isaiah and discover that "the everlasting God, the Lord, the Creator of the ends of the earth, neither faints nor is weary. His understanding is unsearchable. He gives power to the weak, and to those who have no might He increases strength" (verses 28-29).

The attributes of God fill these two verses:

He is eternal—The Everlasting God
He is sovereign—The Lord
He is omnipotent—The Creator of the ends of the earth
He is immutable—He never faints nor is weary
He is omniscient—His understanding is unsearchable
He is merciful—He gives power to the weak
He is gracious—He increases strength to those who have no might

These attributes tell us that God is perfectly capable of getting us where we need to go in His strength. While we're trying to flap our way through life, God is trying to tell us He wants us to soar with Him. Waiting on Him, listening in silence to His Spirit through His Word—that's how we tap into God's attributes and live in His strength.

I want to encourage you to pick out a time and a place to begin being silent before the Lord. Meditate on a portion of His Word and allow it to soak into your heart. You may be able to sit completely in silence for only a couple of minutes at first. But as you get used to meeting with the Lord—to waiting on Him—you will begin to wish you had all day to spend with Him.

In a fascinating article called "The Way of the Eagles," author Bill Britton points out how the mother eagle teaches her little ones to fly. Deuteronomy 32:11 actually paints this picture for us: "As an eagle stirs up its nest, hovers over its young, spreading out its wings, taking them up, carrying them on its wings."

The time comes for the little eagle to strike out on its own and learn to fly, but he fails to see the need. Life is great in the nest! His mother brings him food, he cuddles in a nice secure feather-lined nest . . . what could be better? But the mother begins making things uncomfortable for him—she "stirs up its nest." She breaks twigs so the sharp ends make it impossible for the eaglet to rest. She pulls up the feathery "mattress." This very safe place has suddenly become very uncomfortable.

I wonder if that is not what God does with us. Perhaps He's doing that with you right now—making your comfort zone increasingly uncomfortable so you'll have to step out and trust Him by faith, learn to soar in His strength. Perhaps He's trying to get the word "adventure" back into your vocabulary again.

If stirring up the nest doesn't move the little one to the edge of the nest, the mother eagle begins hovering over the young one, beating her wings. The wings that once protected him from the storm and cold have now become his enemy. In order to escape this discomfort, the little eagle goes to the edge of the nest and climbs upon his mother's back just before she leaps from the nest! Now the two are soaring together in the heavens—until the mother suddenly twists out from under the little eagle. He begins to fall, but instinctively spreads his wings and catches a bit of air.

Just before he is about to crash into the ground, the mother swoops underneath him and bears him up again on her back into the heavens—where she releases him again and again and again until finally he spreads his wings and begins to soar on his own.

My friend, God is in the business of transforming us from hummingbirds who flap to eagles who soar. And He will stop at nothing. His purpose is clear! His children are eagles in the making, destined to soar with the wind of His Spirit under their wings.

Where are you in the process? Are you comfortable in the nest? Are you sitting on the edge of the nest? Are you in a free fall from the back of the mother eagle? Are you starting to soar just a little bit as you begin learning to trust Him?

Learning to soar is about trusting Him. Waiting means trusting. Waiting is saying, "God, I trust You. I'm waiting upon You. I'm believing in You. I'm going to let You guide my life and direct me. I'm turning all that I am over to You. I fully surrender to You. And I will soar on the winds of Your Spirit wherever You want me to go." It's trusting that when He lets you go, you will not fall farther than He wants you to. He will be there to bear you up again, and again, and again, as each time you gain new strength.

Not long before his death, Henri Nouwen wrote a book called *Sabbatical Journey* about some friends of his who were trapeze artists, called the Flying Roudellas. The Roudellas once told Nouwen there is a special relationship between the flyer and the catcher on the trapeze. The flyer is the one that lets go, and the catcher is the one that catches. As the flyer swings high above the crowd on the trapeze, the moment comes when he must let go. He arcs into the air. His job is to remain as still as possible and wait for the strong hands of the catcher to pluck him from the air.

One of the Flying Roudellas told Nouwen, "The flyer must never try to catch the catcher. The flyer must wait in absolute trust."[5] The catcher will catch him—but he must wait.

This is the hardest lesson to learn when it comes to acquiring the courage to live in peace in a frantic world. Isaiah wrote that "those who wait on the Lord shall renew their strength" (verse 31). Are you willing to find a quiet place and a quiet time to begin waiting on God? If you will wait upon Him, He will renew your strength.

You do not have to be a victim of the craziness of the world we live in. Only if you learn to soar above the things of this world in the strength of Almighty God will you be able to live in the peace you need and desire. That is God's will for you. If He is moving you to the edge of the nest, don't resist. Let Him take you with Him to heights you have not known before. Let Him come to you as you wait upon Him.

Notes

1. *San Diego Union,* November 27, 2004, Section B, 1.

2. *USA Today,* July 18, 2000, 1A.

3. Daniel Goleman, *Emotional Intelligence* (Bantam Books, 1997), 80-83.

4. From a sermon preached by Bob Henderson at the Westminster Presbyterian Church, "The Waiting," November 30, 2003, <www.westpreschurch.org/sermons/20031130.pdf>.

5. "Waiting on God," *Preaching Today* #199, In Perfect Illustrations, 283.

1. List the different types of birds mentioned at the beginning of the lesson and describe how each of them fly.

    a. Which bird do you "fly" through life like most of the time?

    b. Why is soaring the best way to "fly" through life?

2. Read Isaiah 40:30-31.

    a. Write out the first phrase of verse 31.

    b. What does waiting on the Lord provide for you according to verse 31?

c. What do you find to be the most difficult part of waiting? Why?

d. In Psalm 24:4-5, what is the psalmist waiting on?

e. What is the result of waiting on the Lord in Psalm 33:20-21?

f. According to Psalm 37:7, what perspective does waiting on the Lord give?

g. In Lamentations 3:25-26, what is the result of waiting on the Lord?

3. Read Isaiah 40:28-29.

   a. How is God described in these verses?

   b. What characteristic of God, as mentioned in these verses, most encourages you today? Why?

   c. Who is the Source of strength for the Christian?

4. In what ways might waiting on the Lord involve stillness and silence? Is being still and silent difficult for you? Why or why not?

5. Describe a time when you have waited on God to renew your strength or give you the guidance or provision you needed. What lessons did you learn during that time?

GROUP QUESTIONS

1. Discuss the three different birds mentioned at the beginning of the lesson and how each of them fly. Share with the group which bird and flying technique you relate to the most and why.

2. Read Isaiah 40:30-31 as a group.

   a. Explain the main principle we learn from these two verses.

   b. In Psalm 25:5, what did the psalmist expect from God?

   c. How is the Lord described in Psalm 33:20-21?

   d. What was the psalmist expecting God to do in Psalm 37:7?

e. According to Lamentations 3:25-26, how can we experience more of God's goodness?

f. Why is waiting difficult for many of us, especially in light of the busyness of our culture today?

3. Read Isaiah 40:28-29.

a. List the different attributes of God mentioned in these verses, along with a description of each attribute.

-

-

-

-

-

-

-

b. Which of the above attributes stands out to you the most? Share with the group why that attribute stands out to you.

c. In what ways does God strengthen us as Christians when we are weak? How have you seen this happen in your own life?

4. Why is it difficult to wait on the Lord in stillness and silence?

5. How do you wait on the Lord on a consistent basis? Share with the group how and when you withdraw from the demands of the day and exercise your hope in the Lord.

DID YOU KNOW?

I saiah wrote that those who wait on the Lord will "renew" their strength (40:31). This is not the kind of renewing that an athlete does—renewing by resting after a strenuous workout. The Hebrew word for "renew," *chalaph,* means (in the particular form used by Isaiah) to change or exchange or substitute one garment for another. It hearkens back to verse 29 where Isaiah says that God "gives power to the weak." Those who have no power exchange their weakness for God's power; they are clothed with God's power. This is a foundational concept for the New Testament where believers are told to "put on the Lord Jesus Christ" (Romans 13:14) and "put on the new self" (Ephesians 4:24, GNT). Those who have no righteousness exchange their lack of righteousness for the righteousness of Christ.

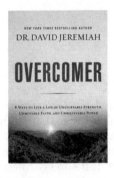

OVERCOMER

In *Overcomer: Eight Ways to Live a Life of Unstoppable Strength, Unmovable Faith, and Unbelievable Power,* Dr. David Jeremiah explores Paul's description of spiritual armor, explaining what it means for Christians to overcome in this world filled with sin and evil. He explains how, when we put on Christ, we have everything we need to stand victorious. You can stand firm against the schemes and strategies of Satan with spiritual armor, and not just stand—but overcome!

SLAYING THE GIANTS IN YOUR LIFE

There's a breed of giants lurking in the shadows, keeping Christians from standing on the promises that accompany their salvation. Who are these giants? Look in our churches and you'll notice fear, discouragement, loneliness, worry, temptation, and guilt. In *Slaying the Giants in Your Life,* Dr. David Jeremiah will help you discover how to recognize and banish these giants from your life!

EVERYTHING YOU NEED

God never intended for us to stumble our way through the course of each day and journey into our future unprepared. He has given us everything we need to walk confidently through life! In *Everything You Need: 8 Essential Steps to a Life of Confidence in the Promises of God*, Dr. Jeremiah examines the words of 2 Peter 1 and shows us how to add diligence, virtue, knowledge, self-control, perseverance, godliness, brotherly kindness, and love to our faith.

FORWARD

Many of us want our life to make a difference, but we aren't sure how to go about accomplishing that. Life's circumstances can weigh us down and prevent us from living the life we desire. In *Forward*, Dr. Jeremiah will take you through Scripture and teach you how to discover God's purpose for your life and move forward in it. God has a plan for your life!

Each of these resources was created from a teaching series by Dr. David Jeremiah. Contact Turning Point for more information about correlating materials.

For pricing information and ordering, contact us at

P.O. Box 3838
San Diego, CA 92163
(800) 947-1993
www.DavidJeremiah.org

STAY CONNECTED
to Dr. David Jeremiah

Take advantage of two great ways to let Dr. David Jeremiah give you spiritual direction every day!

Turning Points Magazine and Devotional

Receive Dr. David Jeremiah's magazine, *Turning Points*, each month:

- Thematic study focus
- 52 pages of life-changing reading
- Relevant articles
- Special features
- Daily devotional readings
- Bible study resource offers
- Live event schedule
- Radio & television information

Request *Turning Points* magazine today!

(800) 947-1993
www.DavidJeremiah.org/Magazine

Daily Turning Point E-Devotional

Start your day off right! Find words of inspiration and spiritual motivation waiting for you on your computer every morning! Receive a daily e-devotion communication from David Jeremiah that will strengthen your walk with God and encourage you to live the authentic Christian life.

Request your free e-devotional today!

(800) 947-1993
www.DavidJeremiah.org/Devo